The Trail of Tears

REMOVAL IN THE SOUTH

LANDMARK EVENTS IN
NATIVE AMERICAN HISTORY

THE APACHE WARS
The Final Resistance

BLACK HAWK AND THE WAR OF 1832
Removal in the North

CODE TALKERS AND WARRIORS
Native Americans and World War II

KING PHILIP'S WAR
The Conflict Over New England

LITTLE BIGHORN
Winning the Battle, Losing the War

THE LONG WALK
The Forced Navajo Exile

RED POWER
The Native American Civil Rights Movement

THE TRAIL OF TEARS
Removal in the South

The Trail of Tears

REMOVAL IN THE SOUTH

JOHN P. BOWES
Assistant Professor of History
Eastern Kentucky University

SERIES EDITOR: PAUL C. ROSIER
Assistant Professor of History
Villanova University

CHELSEA HOUSE
PUBLISHERS
An imprint of Infobase Publishing

Cover: Known as the Trail of Tears, the forced march of the Cherokees in 1838–39 is depicted in this oil painting by American artist Robert Lindneux.

THE TRAIL OF TEARS: Removal in the South

Copyright © 2007 by Infobase Publishing

Chelsea House
An imprint of Infobase Publishing
132 West 31st Street
New York NY 10001

Library of Congress Cataloging-in-Publication Data
Bowes, John P., 1973-
The Trail of Tears : removal in the south / John P. Bowes.
   p. cm. — (Landmark Events in Native American History)
Includes bibliographical references and index.
ISBN-13: 978-0-7910-9345-0 (hardcover)
ISBN-10: 0-7910-9345-X (hardcover)
 1. Trail of Tears, 1838. 2. Cherokee Indians—Relocation. 3. Cherokee Indians—Government policy. 4. Cherokee Nation, Oklahoma. Treaties, etc. United States, 1835 Dec. 29. I. Title.
E99.C5B746 2007
975.004′97557—dc22   2006102274

Chelsea House books are available at special discounts when purchased in bulk quantities for businesses, associations, institutions, or sales promotions. Please call our Special Sales Department in New York at (212) 967-8800 or (800) 322-8755.

You can find Chelsea House on the World Wide Web at
http://www.chelseahouse.com

Series design by Erika K. Arroyo
Cover design by Ben Peterson
Illustrations by Sholto Ainslie

Printed in the United States of America

Bang FOF 10 9 8 7 6 5 4 3 2 1

This book is printed on acid-free paper.

All links and Web addresses were checked and verified to be correct at the time of publication. Because of the dynamic nature of the Web, some addresses and links may have changed since publication and may no longer be valid.

Contents

The Context of Indian Removal North and South

On a cold December day in 1830, President Andrew Jackson spoke to Congress and celebrated the passage of the Indian Removal Act. Six months earlier, Congress had voted in favor of that landmark bill. It gave authority to the president and his representatives to negotiate for Indian lands as well as the removal of all Indians living east of the Mississippi River. Jackson supported the bill and made sure that it overcame any opposition in Congress. But Indian removal was not his idea. The seeds of this legislation had been planted years earlier. Ideas about land, civilization, and American Indians in the early 1800s helped lead to the Indian Removal Act.

The desire for land was the primary reason for Indian removal. In the early 1600s, English settlers established colonies at Jamestown, Plymouth, and other locations. They eventually fought with local Indian populations over the presence and extension of those settlements. Periods of peace did occur during the next two centuries. Europeans and Indians lived near each other and traded food, animal skins, and other material goods. But still, the forceful extension of European colonies and Indian resistance to that expansion continued. By the time the American colonists rebelled against the British government in the 1770s, most eastern Indians had been pushed farther inland. In the early 1800s, the United States negotiated numerous treaties with Indian tribes. Under these agreements, the Indians gave up even more of their land. All told, these treaties arranged for the transfer of millions of acres from Indian to American ownership.

The Louisiana Purchase of 1803 marked an important turning point. This event drastically changed Americans' visions of their country and the eastern Indian communities. For $15 million, the Jefferson administration bought from the French a vast region of land west of the Mississippi River, thus more than doubling the size of the United States. President Thomas Jefferson believed that this western territory provided a solution to the problem confronting the U.S. government and its citizens. Tens of thousands of Indians continued to occupy lands between the Appalachian Mountains and the Mississippi River. Jefferson proposed that the Louisiana Territory could provide a new home to these people, who in his mind represented an obstacle to American expansion. In public statements, the president even stated that removal would be a noble policy. The federal government would be helping the Indians, who had already suffered so much from the presence of white Americans on their lands.

Jefferson was not the only one who spoke about removal as a positive development for American Indians. In the early 1800s, most white Americans were convinced that the Indians could not survive the changes brought about by colonization. Tens of thousands of Indians had died from smallpox and other diseases the colonists had brought with them from Europe. Indian men and women continued to resist attempts by Christian missionaries to change their way of life. The introduction of alcohol, declining animal populations, and colonial trade goods had increased Indian dependence on

During Thomas Jefferson's first term as president, the United States purchased the 828,000-square-mile (2,145,000-square-kilometer) Louisiana Territory from France for less than three cents per acre. Jefferson believed that this vast territory was an ideal home for the Indian tribes of the East and thus supported their removal from their traditional lands.

white Americans and hurt their ability to survive in traditional ways.

As a result, most Americans believed that both the Indians and their way of life were destined to disappear. With the removal legislation, government officials gave the Indians a choice of fates. They could adopt a lifestyle more similar to white Americans and stay where they were, or they could give up their eastern lands and move west of the Mississippi River. Either way, the Indian presence would be removed from the eastern territories.

That vision matched the theme of one of the most popular books of the early nineteenth century, *The Last of the Mohicans*. In the final paragraph of that novel, the Delaware chief Tamenund spoke over the grave of the Mohican warrior Uncas. "The pale faces are masters of the earth," Tamenund declared, "and the time of the red men has not yet come again."[1] Like Uncas and Tamenund, eastern Indians were expected to die or submit peacefully to the needs of white Americans.

LEGAL AND LEGISLATIVE FOUNDATIONS FOR REMOVAL

Indian removal was based on more than just opinions about civilization and the vanishing Indian. It also grew out of European history and past U.S. Supreme Court decisions. After the American Revolution, the government officials created an Indian policy based on treaties and the doctrine of discovery, relying on the tradition of their European forefathers.

The American Revolution officially ended with the Treaty of Paris in 1783. At that point, the new government of the United States had to decide how to deal with the Indian tribes living inside and outside the boundaries of the 13 states. The United States first took a strong position. Officials argued that the Indians, especially those in the Ohio Valley, deserved punishment for allying with the British during the war. But these officials soon realized they could not be so forceful. First, the Indians in the Ohio Valley disagreed with the American stance. Second, the United States did not have the military and economic strength to enforce such punishment. Instead, the young government needed to protect its newly won independence by establishing peace.

In 1789, Secretary of War Henry Knox recommended that the United States pursue negotiations with the northern and southern Indian tribes by recognizing their "right to the soil." This policy meant that the federal government could only obtain Indian land "by their free consent, or by the right of conquest in case of a just war."[2] From that point forward, the treaty became the basis of Indian policy. Each treaty was a legal document that transferred the right to the soil from Indians to the U.S. government.

A legal ruling made by the U.S. Supreme Court in 1823 strengthened this policy. Chief Justice John Marshall, in his decision in the case of *Johnson v. McIntosh*, reaffirmed the doctrine of discovery. This doctrine dated back to the age of European exploration, 50 years before Christopher Columbus sailed from the shores of Spain. In brief, the pope in Rome, whose power ruled over the decisions made by many countries at the time, gave European explorers the right to claim ownership of land in the name of their respective countries. According to the doctrine, each explorer could do this without any regard for the presence or claims of local native populations.

Chief Justice Marshall outlined the transfer of ownership in North America based on this doctrine. Prior to the American Revolution, the British had asserted a claim to Indian lands from the Atlantic Ocean to the Mississippi River. Because of this assertion, the Indians did not own any land under control of the British. From a European legal perspective, the Indians only had the right to occupy it. After the revolution, the United States through their military victory inherited the British land claims. This was known as the right of conquest. Marshall argued that the U.S. government now had the exclusive right to erase Indian claims to the land.

These legal foundations of Indian policy made two points clear. First, the federal government would be the sole mediator in land matters. Only treaties negotiated by federal officials would be legitimate. These signed documents would therefore represent an agreement between nations. Second, though the U.S. government proposed to bargain for Indian lands through treaties, it would not recognize Indian ownership of the land. The right of occupancy gave the Indians only minimal claims. More important, the United States could simply remove the Indians from the land if necessary.

REGIONAL CONTEXTS OF REMOVAL

The ideas and policies supporting Indian removal did not have the same impact throughout the country. From the Ohio Valley to Georgia, white Americans had different reasons for supporting removal legislation. In the northern states, the conflicts of the late 1700s and early 1800s, as well as the desire for land, made settlers in the region push for the removal of the Potawatomis, Shawnees, Delawares, and Wyandots. A similar desire for land as well as the rise of cotton growing fueled calls for the removal of Cherokees, Creeks, and Choctaws in the southern states.

In the late 1780s, the Shawnee, Miami, Potawatomi, and other Indian tribes in the Old Northwest formed a military alliance against American expansion. They wanted to make sure that white settlements stayed south of the Ohio River. In a number of councils that included representatives from tribes in the Great Lakes region and the Southeast, Indian leaders formed a strong alliance against the United States. Two different American armies suffered significant defeats in the early 1790s before General Anthony Wayne finally subdued the Indian confederates at the Battle of Fallen Timbers (near present-day Toledo, Ohio) in 1794. The Treaty of Greenville officially ended that conflict in 1795. In that agreement, the northern Indians surrendered most of present-day Ohio.

The northern Indians united again in the early 1800s under the leadership of two Shawnee Indians. In 1806, the Shawnee prophet Tenskwatawa began to preach against the evils of the white man's ways. He told his followers to reject the material goods and Christianity of the Americans. His brother Tecumseh was the political leader of this alliance. Tecumseh traveled throughout the eastern half of the United States to rally resistance to the intrusions of American settlers. This confederacy also suffered defeat. The most significant loss occurred in 1811, when an army under William Henry Harrison attacked and overwhelmed the Indian forces at the Battle of Tippecanoe (in present-day west-central Indiana).

The end of this unified military resistance had two results. First, the military defeats led to treaties that established peace and opened lands to white settlement. By the late 1810s, thousands of settlers had flooded the Ohio Valley and lands farther west. Enough Americans moved into the region that Ohio, Indiana, and Illinois gained statehood between 1803 and 1818. The increased settlement in the region escalated the calls to negotiate for Indian lands. By the mid-1820s, most of the Delawares and Shawnees had already signed treaties, left the Ohio Valley, and crossed the Mississippi. The Miamis, Potawatomis, Ottawas, and Wyandots who remained were under constant pressure to surrender their claims to the land.

A second and equally important impact of the military conflicts in the early 1800s had to do with the American public's ideas about Indians. Americans believed, in part, that the Indians' resistance to the settlement of the Ohio Valley showed that they would never change. Tecumseh gained a heroic reputation among Americans after his death, but it was because he had fought nobly and did not compromise his beliefs. He had been a worthy enemy. However, after his death in 1813, he and his people were considered to be a part of history. In short, many white residents of the Ohio Valley and elsewhere did not believe that whites and Indians could

When the Shawnee chief Tecumseh was killed at the Battle of the Thames during the War of 1812, many Ohio Valley residents believed it signaled the demise of the American Indian in that part of the country. Tecumseh (center) is depicted here challenging U.S. colonel Richard M. Johnson at the Battle of the Thames on October 5, 1813.

peacefully coexist. Removal, therefore, would be the best way to handle any Indians who still claimed land in the region.

The desire for land also fueled demands for removal in the Southeast. Citizens and officials of southern states attempted to obtain as much Indian territory as possible in the decades after the American Revolution. However, the push for land in the 1800s was more directly attached to the development of cotton as a cash crop. Agriculture supported by slave labor became the core of the southern economy in the early nineteenth century. Perhaps more than any other factor this development helps explain the support for Indian removal in the region.

Many southeastern Indian tribes suffered great losses during the American Revolution. Among the Cherokees, a militant leader named Dragging Canoe pushed for an alliance with the British against the colonists. This support for the British grew out of the rising anger against colonists who had begun to extend their settlements into Indian territories. In the late 1760s and early 1770s, Dragging Canoe and other like-minded Cherokees had participated in numerous councils with Shawnee leaders and other Ohio Indians who shared their beliefs. But the Cherokee alliance with the British quickly proved problematic when the colonists took military action. From the middle of July to the end of October 1776, militias from Virginia, North Carolina, and South Carolina launched at least four different expeditions into Cherokee country. The results were disastrous for the Cherokees. Hundreds of them were killed and the colonial militias burned crops and buildings in nearly 50 towns.

These initial losses led most Cherokees to negotiate a peace with American colonists in 1777. Dragging Canoe and his followers, known as the Chickamaugas, continued to resist. Yet for the most part, Cherokee participation in the American Revolution ended in that first year. Once the conflict ended, the newly independent U.S. government focused its military efforts in the Ohio Valley. In the Southeast, federal officials chose to negotiate treaties to maintain the peace. The most prominent aspect of this effort by U.S. officials involved numerous attempts to ensure that settlers would respect Indian boundaries.

However, the interests of individual states complicated relations between the federal government and American Indians. In the 1780s, the United States operated under the Articles of Confederation, a precursor to today's U.S. Constitution. The articles established a weak central government and granted significant authority to the states. Indeed, both North Carolina and Georgia took advantage of this fact and forced the Cherokees to give up portions of their land to settlers in the years after the end of the American

Revolution. The Cherokees could not believe that the states had the authority to take territory so easily.

Although the federal government gained new strength with the creation and ratification of the U.S. Constitution, the situation for the Cherokees changed only slightly. In the Treaty of Holston, signed in 1791, federal officials declared that any U.S. citizen or non-Indian who thereafter settled on Cherokee lands would forfeit the protection of the federal government. This promise to protect boundaries coincided with a push for further land cessions. Between 1798 and 1806, Cherokee leaders signed five different treaties with the U.S. government that ceded territory in Tennessee, Georgia, Alabama, and North Carolina.

Events during the War of 1812 advanced the push to obtain Indian lands in the Southeast. A civil war within the Creek Nation broke out when a group of conservative Creeks turned against those who had begun to move away from a traditional lifestyle. The more conservative Creeks were called the Red Sticks, and attacks by them on other Creek settlements raised fears among local U.S. citizens of an Indian uprising. Andrew Jackson, a major general of the Tennessee Militia at the time, gathered a force made up of Americans, Cherokees, and Creeks. He led this army against the Red Sticks and defeated them at the Battle of Horseshoe Bend (near present-day Wetumpka, Alabama) in 1814. After the battle, General Jackson imposed a treaty on the entire Creek Nation. Under the terms of this treaty, the Creeks gave up approximately 23 million acres of land that included large portions of Georgia and Alabama.

Jackson's imposition of the 1814 treaty reflected more than just a desire for more land for settlers. Even before this battle against the Creeks, farmers in the South had begun to plant cotton in greater numbers than ever before. As a crop, cotton is difficult to process and tough on the soil. But the invention of the cotton gin in 1793 presented a solution to the first problem by making it easier to separate the seeds from the cotton fibers. This in turn led to an increased production of cotton, as well as an increased reliance on African-American slave labor in the fields.

Yet little could be done to change the way that cotton drained nutrients from the soil. To accommodate the desire of planters to expand their cotton production, it was necessary to obtain more land. As it happened, the fertile soil in Georgia and the territory that became Alabama and Mississippi was well suited to cotton. The 1814 treaty with the Creeks therefore opened up much of that desirable land to settlement. Established planters and hopeful settlers quickly took advantage of this opportunity. Between 1816 and 1820, tens of thousands of settlers entered the region. The population of Alabama alone skyrocketed from 9,046 in 1810 to 127,901 in 1820. These eager masses demanded that the U.S. government open up more land. The Creeks, Choctaws, Chickasaws, and Cherokees stood in their way.

CONCLUSION

In the Great Lakes region and the Southeast in the late eighteenth and early nineteenth centuries, the Shawnee, Cherokee, and other Indian tribes struggled to deal with the invasion of U.S. settlers. From the American Revolution onward, they faced a young U.S. government that tried to contain its citizens even as it negotiated treaties that arranged for land cessions. In the end, although the specific circumstances of conflicts over land in each region were different, the calls for removal by the 1820s were very similar.

Overall, two distinct factors set the stage for the passage of the Indian Removal Act in 1830. First, both the Europeans and the Americans had an overwhelming desire for land. From the early 1600s to the early 1800s, their settlements extended farther inland into Indian territories. Treaties and

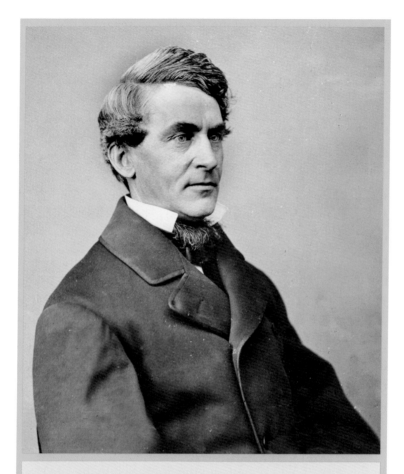

Senator Theodore Frelinghuysen of New Jersey was the leading opponent to the U.S. government's removal policy. During the Senate's Indian removal debate in April 1830, Frelinghuysen delivered a six-hour speech condemning the act and warning of its potential pitfalls.

legal rulings supported these actions. An official removal policy appeared to be the next logical step. The second factor rested on the assumed inferiority of Indian peoples. People of the United States believed that Indian individuals and tribes could not survive the advance of Western civilization and were therefore destined to disappear. Relocation would make that future a reality. It would remove them from the lands and lives of settlers living east of the Mississippi River.

Yet even with these sentiments, the Indian Removal Act did not become law without controversy. Organizations throughout the country, and especially in the Northeast, argued against the legislation. Within the halls of Congress, senators and state representatives vehemently opposed the idea of removal and decried the greed of U.S. citizens. Senator Theodore Frelinghuysen of New Jersey gave one of the more impassioned speeches. "We have crowded the tribes upon a few miserable acres on our southern frontier," he proclaimed. "[It] is all that is left to them of their once boundless forests: and still, like the horse-leech, our insatiated cupidity cries, give! give!"[3] Frelinghuysen had many allies in both the House of Representatives and the Senate, but they fell short in their effort to block the bill. The House passed the Indian Removal Act by a vote of 102 to 97, and the Senate concurred by a similar margin.

President Andrew Jackson did not address that controversy, nor did he mention the desire for land or the inferiority of Indians in such a direct manner in his speech to Congress on December 6, 1830. Instead he described Indian removal in a positive light. But his use of words like *generous* and *kindly* could not hide the fact that this policy was based more on the desire for more land than on concern for the future of eastern Indian tribes.

The Cherokees
and Georgia

UNTIL THE LAND CESSION TREATIES OF THE LATE 1700S
and early 1800s, Cherokee territory spread over a significant
portion of the Southeast. The Cherokees had established
settlements throughout the land that is now encompassed by
western North Carolina, western South Carolina, northern
Georgia, northeastern Alabama, and eastern Tennessee. However, warfare, settler encroachment, and negotiated accords
had gradually diminished the extent of the Cherokee land.
By the third decade of the nineteenth century, much of the
Cherokee Nation rested within the boundaries of the state of
Georgia. This circumstance set the stage for the central political and legal battle in the years prior to the Trail of Tears.

The Cherokee Nation and the state of Georgia initiated
a political standoff in 1827. In July of that year, the Cherokees ratified and proclaimed their newly written constitution.
It was modeled after the U.S. Constitution and established
three branches of government. Just as important, this document and its principles announced the determination of the
Cherokees to maintain their status as an independent nation.

Five months later, the Georgia state legislature responded to the Cherokees' actions. In a limited but critical move, Georgia officials extended the jurisdiction of certain county courts over crimes against or by white citizens on Cherokee lands. The point was clear. Georgia wanted to affirm the authority of the state's institutions and laws over those of the Cherokees.

The events of 1827 highlighted two important developments that affected the struggle over removal in the next decade. First, the stance taken by the Cherokee government meant that much of the debate would occur in the areas of law and politics. Though physical confrontations and conflict played a role in the events that followed, the crucial decisions were made in government buildings and courtrooms. Second, and most important, the struggle over removal was not just about Cherokees living on lands that Georgia settlers wanted. It was about who had the authority to rule over that territory. Georgia wanted to control all of the land within its state boundaries, and the Cherokees wanted to maintain authority over the land on which they lived.

FOUNDATIONS OF THE CHEROKEE CONSTITUTION

The Cherokee Constitution of 1827 signaled two developments. First, it represented the culmination of decades of change within Cherokee culture. Second, it marked the beginning of a new phase of Cherokee government. By the early nineteenth century, the Cherokees' traditional politics had altered considerably. These political changes reflected many of the economic and cultural changes within Cherokee society during the same period. Yet the institution of their new constitution also made a dramatic political statement. The document indicated the firm belief of the Cherokees in the autonomy of their nation.

The centralized government set up by the 1827 constitution was vastly different from the traditional tribal government

CONSTITUTION

OF THE

CHEROKEE NATION,

MADE AND ESTABLISHED

AT A

GENERAL CONVENTION OF DELEGATES,

DULY AUTHORISED FOR THAT PURPOSE,

AT

NEW ECHOTA,

JULY 26, 1827.

———

PRINTED FOR THE CHEROKEE NATION,
AT THE OFFICE OF THE STATESMAN AND PATRIOT,
GEORGIA.

In 1827, the Cherokee Nation ratified its first constitution, which promoted the Cherokees' belief that they were indeed a sovereign nation. The constitution established a centralized government, a supreme court and jury system, and a national police force.

of the past. Into the late eighteenth century, clan relations, town-based authority, and religious leaders played substantial roles in Cherokee governance. Instead of a single government that oversaw a unified nation, individual village councils provided the necessary political and legal structures and rulings. The Cherokees were a matrilineal society, which meant that they traced their descent and kinship through women instead of men. This kinship system granted women an influential role in their communities, including politics. Both men and women voiced their opinions in their village councils and participated equally in the decision-making process. That process itself depended on consensus. All participants had to agree before a decision became final.

However, the impact of trade and other interactions with European settlers and missionaries altered these traditions over time. Interrelated economic and cultural changes had a direct effect on the nature of Cherokee government. In the late 1700s, the Cherokees were active participants in the lucrative deerskin trade. Cherokee men traveled throughout the Southeast to hunt the deer and Cherokee women worked hard to cure the skins requested by British traders. But excessive hunting by the Cherokees and other Indians diminished the deer population to a tremendous extent. The colonial wars of the mid-eighteenth century also took their toll on the lives of Indians in the Southeast. As the Cherokees recovered from their losses after the American Revolution, they sought a new means for their survival.

The Cherokees' search for a new economic foundation coincided with the efforts of the U.S. government to promote "civilization" among the Indians. Government officials hoped the transformation of Indian hunters into Indian farmers would ease the process of assimilation into U.S. society. Missionaries were one of the important elements of this effort. The Cherokees were eager to make up for the decline of the deerskin trade and wanted to establish more peaceful relations with the United States. They therefore welcomed the Christian missionaries who established schools in their nation in the early 1800s.

This emphasis on education had a clear impact on the younger members of the Cherokee Nation. By the 1820s, significant numbers of boys and girls attended schools run by Moravians, Methodists, and other Christian denominations. Not only did these children learn to read and write, but they also listened to the missionaries' lessons about civilization. Some Cherokee youths, like Sally M. Reece, began to share these ideas about progress. In July 1828, she wrote a letter discussing the situation of her people: "I think they improve," she observed. "They have a printing press, and print a paper which is called the Cherokee Phoenix. They come to meeting on Sabbath days. They wear clothes which they made themselves."[4] The paper she mentioned, the *Cherokee Phoenix*, was the first newspaper ever published by an Indian nation. This paper was only one element mentioned by Reece, and in the rest of her letter she listed several ways in which the Cherokees had improved by leaving their old practices behind.

One point that Reece did not mention in her letter was that the *Cherokee Phoenix* was published in both English and Cherokee. In 1821, a Cherokee named Sequoyah introduced a Cherokee syllabary, which broke down the spoken language into 86 different written symbols. This development not only assisted the education of children in schools, but also spawned a literacy movement throughout the Cherokee Nation. Adults as well as children could soon read in both English and Cherokee.

There were a number of consequences of the Christian missionaries' emphasis on farming over hunting and the transition to a lifestyle more dependent on agriculture. Women had always been responsible for the agricultural production in Cherokee villages. Although men would help out with

(continues on page 28)

THE *CHEROKEE PHOENIX*

The *Cherokee Phoenix* was the first newspaper published by an American Indian tribe. On February 21, 1828, the first edition rolled off the printing press that had been purchased by the Cherokees the previous year. Every edition was printed in both Cherokee and English. The Cherokee government used the paper to communicate official news, laws, and other developments to Cherokees living throughout the Southeast. Non-Cherokees also read the paper, which meant that the Cherokees could also use the *Phoenix* to address U.S. citizens and officials. As the paper's editor, Elias Boudinot therefore had the opportunity to comment on circumstances within the Cherokee Nation and developments beyond its borders. In the late 1820s, one of the most notable situations was the conflict between the Cherokees and Georgia. When the Cherokees proclaimed the adoption of their new constitution, many outsiders refused to believe that the Cherokees could have drafted this document without the assistance of white missionaries. Boudinot wrote the following response to these attacks and it appeared in the *Phoenix* on March 20, 1828.

We were not a little diverted, in noticing lately, in a paper, to which we are not now able to recur, a motion made in the House of Representatives, by Mr. Wilde, a member from Georgia, to take measures to ascertain what white persons have assisted the Cherokees in forming the late constitution; and in what way, and to what extent, such assistance has been afforded. It is a little surprising that in almost every instance, wherein the Indians have undertaken to imitate their white brethren, and have succeeded . . . it is currently noised about, that all is imposition, as though Indians were incapable of performing the deeds of their white neighbours. This evidences an extreme prejudice. We cannot conceive to ourselves, what benefit Mr. Wilde expected to receive

(continues)

(continued)

CHEROKEE PHŒNIX

VOL. I.   NEW ECHOTA, THURSDAY FEBRUARY 21, 1828.   NO. I.

in offering such a motion, or who are the persons that are suspected of having interfered in this affair? We believe that the Cherokees are as scrupulous, in avoiding such interference, as Mr. W. if not more so.

It has been customary of late to charge the Missionaries with the crime of assisting the Indians, and unbecomingly interfering in political affairs; and as some of these are the only white persons (with few exceptions) in this Nation, who are capable of affording any substantial assistance, it is probable Mr. W. had a direct reference to them. We can, however, assure him, that . . . the Cherokees will not, by any means, permit them to have any thing to do with their public affairs, and we believe, that as their sole object is to afford religious instruction, the societies under which they labour particularly forbid their interference in political matters. . . . They have our hearty approbation for what they have done amongst us, and we hope those at a distance will reward them by their kind wishes and sympathies, instead of affixing to them the term of "mercenary missionaries." They certainly deserve better treatment. Perhaps this short article will be considered an imposition by such persons as are wont to judge at a distance and without evidence, and as nothing more than a Missionary's own defence.

Our object, when we commenced to pen this article, was to correct the mistake, under which some may labour, and to declare once and for all, that no white man has had any thing to do in framing our constitution, and all the public acts of the Nation. The Cherokees only are accountable for them, and they certainly do not wish to have any innocent person implicated wrongfully. We hope this practice of imputing the acts of Indians to white men will be done away.

(opposite page) The *Cherokee Phoenix* was the first newspaper published by Native Americans in the United States. The first edition, pictured here, was printed on February 21, 1828.

In 1809, Sequoyah set out to create a system of writing for the Cherokees to help them maintain their independence. Sequoyah completed his 86-symbol syllabary in 1821 and it was quickly adopted by the Cherokees, who used it in their schools, newspapers, and books.

(continued from page 24)

various aspects of the planting and harvesting, the labor of providing vegetables for sustenance rested primarily on the shoulders of Cherokee women. Men made their contribution to the survival of their families by hunting the deer, turkeys, and bears that roamed the nearby woodlands. Together, the labor of Cherokee women and men provided for the daily needs of their people.

The lifestyle emphasized by the missionaries put men in the fields and women in the homes, roles that were different from Cherokee norms. Many struggled to accommodate these new gender roles even as they believed that change was necessary for their survival. Some men compromised by raising livestock while their wives tended their subsistence gardens. This allowed the Cherokees to appease U.S. officials even as they stayed relatively close to their traditional roles.

Although most Cherokees made changes that did not dramatically alter their lifestyle, some families relied on the labor of slaves in the fields and in the home. Throughout the Southeast in the early 1800s, the success of cotton as a cash crop was dependent on the rise of African-American slavery. Within a short period of time, the Cherokee population included a growing number of wealthy planters who shared in this trend. One of the wealthier individuals, a man by the name of John Ridge, described the status and circumstances of his fellow Cherokees who owned slaves. "In this class," he commented, "the principal value of property is retained and their farms are conducted in the same style with the southern white farmers of equal ability in point of property."[5] Although slave owners did not comprise the majority of Cherokees, they did, like their white counterparts, represent an influential minority.

Many members of this growing Cherokee elite were men of mixed descent, sons of unions between Indian women and European traders. By the early 1800s, the Cherokees had dealt with European traders for nearly two centuries. Those years of interaction had resulted in more than just the addition of new material goods to Cherokee culture. Over time, both sexual relations and marriage, primarily between male traders and female Cherokees, had led to significant numbers of mixed-descent individuals within the Cherokee population. In fact, an 1835 federal government census of the Cherokees living east of the Mississippi River reported that nearly one out of every four Cherokees had a mixed heritage.

Because most of these men and women of mixed heritage had Cherokee mothers, they were members of the Cherokee Nation by descent. However, the influence of their Euro-American fathers also contributed to their attitudes toward cultural change. Many mixed-descent men and women of this economic elite believed strongly that the Cherokees as a community needed both to welcome and encourage the programs encouraged by U.S. officials and missionaries. They felt that this would show the United States that the Indians wanted to live in peace with white settlers. With every passing year in the early nineteenth century, many mixed-descent men in particular grew more influential in the political life of the Cherokee Nation.

Their influence led to several key adjustments in the years leading up to the drafting of the Cherokee Constitution. More and more, the voices listened to in councils were those belonging to men. This transition reflected the increased interaction with missionaries and federal officials, who expected men to be in positions of leadership. At the same time, the effort to conform to what whites deemed to be progress affected the very structure of Cherokee government. In 1808, the first written law of the Cherokee Nation established a national police force to protect the property of individual Cherokees. Two years later, another law reserved the national government's right to punish murderers. Then, in 1817, the Cherokee National Council ruled that only that national body had the authority to cede lands. With every law put in place, the Cherokees further centralized their government and laid the foundation for the Cherokee Constitution of 1827.

In brief, the Cherokee Constitution set up a government structure similar to that of the United States. The legislative branch consisted of two different bodies—the General Council and the National Council. Cherokee voters from eight districts elected the members of these bodies. In a clear sign that certain elements of traditional politics were disappearing, only free Cherokee males could vote and only free Cherokee males were eligible for political office. The members of the General Council then selected the officers of the executive branch. Those executive offices included a principal chief, an assistant principal chief, a treasurer, and three counselors. A Supreme Court of three judges oversaw a judicial branch that encompassed any and all district courts within the nation.

Just as important, however, was that by creating the constitution, the Cherokee people were sending a direct message to Georgia and the United States about Cherokee independence and sovereignty. If nothing else, the framers of this constitution made it clear that the Cherokee Nation was not going to concede political authority to any outside power. Although they were willing to alter their traditional form of politics, they would not surrender their independence.

The dual message of this document was laid out in the first few sections. The first article began with a reference to the boundaries of the Cherokee Nation. These boundaries were "guaranteed and reserved forever" by treaty and "shall forever hereafter remain unalterably the same." A lengthy description of those specific borders followed. The beginning of the second section of that first article affirmed the powers of the Cherokee Nation. "The sovereignty & jurisdiction of this Government," it declared, "shall extend over the country with in the boundaries above described."

In those statements, the framers of the Cherokee Constitution made two distinct points. First, the lands on which the Cherokees resided were guaranteed to the Cherokees. Therefore, only the Cherokees could decide if they would cede those lands; no one else had a say. Second, the Cherokees declared that their independent government had sole authority over the lands within those boundaries, and therefore, sole political power resided in the hands of the Cherokees.

As part of the language of the 1827 constitution, the Cherokees claimed that the land upon which they resided was guaranteed to them. Therefore, they were the only ones who could cede the land to the U.S. government. Pictured here is an 1826 map of Georgia that details the Cherokees' territory in the northwestern part of the state.

GEORGIA AND STATE RIGHTS

Officials from the state of Georgia were not pleased with the Cherokee referral to their land as "guaranteed and reserved forever." However, Georgians were even more upset with the Cherokee declaration of sovereignty. The existence of an independent nation within the boundaries of the state was deemed unacceptable. According to Georgia, the state government should have authority over all people and lands within its boundaries. For Georgia, then, this battle with the Cherokees was as much about political power as it was about resistance to removal.

From the American Revolution forward, Georgia displayed a strong commitment to its rights as a state within the union. In 1793, in fact, state officials challenged the power of the newly established U.S. Supreme Court. Attorneys for the state refused to argue before the court in a case stemming from economic transactions during the American Revolution. They asserted that the Supreme Court did not have the authority to order the sovereign state of Georgia to appear. In the final ruling on *Chisholm v. Georgia*, the Supreme Court justices ruled in favor of the plaintiff and against Georgia. Nevertheless, Georgia did not back down from its belief in the rights of individual states.

The next point of contention involved Georgia's western land claims. In the late eighteenth century, the U.S. government asserted control over western expansion. To do so, it needed each state to relinquish any claims to lands beyond its present boundaries. Georgia's royal charter of 1732 granted the state all of the territory from the Atlantic Ocean to the Mississippi River. Georgia was the last of the original 13 states to give up its western claim.

Georgia negotiated a critical agreement in exchange for the land in question. This accord was known as the Compact of 1802. It created a binding agreement between the state of Georgia and the federal government. Georgia gave up its claims to all land west of its present boundaries. In exchange, the federal government agreed to extinguish all Indian land claims within the state. This territory would then be turned over to Georgia. The compact did not set a timetable for this action, but it did commit the federal government to remove the Indians "as early as the same can be peaceably obtained, upon reasonable terms."

Georgia did not press the issue in the first two decades after the negotiation of the compact. The War of 1812 created more important concerns in the region. It also helped that Andrew Jackson obtained approximately 23 million acres of land from the Creeks in the Treaty of Fort Jackson in 1814. This cession opened up some of the most fertile land within the state and appeased Georgians for the time being. They showed little concern about the failure of the federal government to extinguish the Cherokee land claims.

However, treaties signed with the Cherokees in 1817 and 1819 reminded Georgians about the promises made in the Compact of 1802. The 1817 accord indicated a split among the Cherokees in Georgia. Specifically, Cherokees of the so-called lower towns on the Hiwassee River wished to move west of the Mississippi River because they did not agree with the cultural changes that had taken place. Instead of relying on agriculture, they wanted to continue their traditional lifestyle and believed that only relocation would allow them the freedom to do so. As part of this 1817 accord, these Cherokees obtained western lands, but only through the cession of territory along the Apalachee and Chattahoochee rivers. In the 1819 treaty, the Cherokees surrendered even more land. From Georgia's perspective, these cessions were not enough and only reminded state citizens and officials of the federal government's unfulfilled promise. And while Indian removal was the ultimate goal, the partial relocation in 1817 further highlighted the presence of the approximately 16,000 Cherokees who remained.

Therefore, when the Cherokees announced their constitution in July 1827, the state of Georgia believed it needed to take action. It had become apparent that the federal government was not going to assert its authority over the Cherokees. Georgia officials refused to allow an Indian tribe living within the state borders to declare itself an independent nation. The first move, in December 1827, extended the jurisdiction of certain county courts adjacent to the Cherokee lands. That was only the beginning.

Two years later, in December 1829, Georgia established a much more extreme position. The state legislature wrote and passed an act that extended all Georgia laws over Cherokee lands. It divided Cherokee lands and added that territory to the five adjacent counties. More important, the act annulled "all laws and ordinances made by the Cherokee nation of Indians." According to Georgia state law, the Cherokee Nation did not exist as a political entity.

With laws passed in 1827 and 1829, Georgia made a direct response to the Cherokee Constitution. State officials refused to acknowledge the position held by the Cherokees. From their perspective, the existence of an independent Indian nation within the state borders went against the very principles they had fought for since the American Revolution. The federal government had not acted on the Compact of 1802. As a result, Georgia took action to assert its right as a sovereign state.

CONCLUSION

The struggles between Georgia and the Cherokees in the late 1820s set up a complicated series of power struggles. Each government asserted its authority and proclaimed its sovereignty. The Cherokee declaration was both the culmination of changes within the nation and the belief that such an assertion was necessary. The Cherokees needed to declare their intention to remain on their lands. Georgia's actions reflected a similar combination of events. It asserted its state rights as it had throughout the previous decades. But it also acted because it felt it was necessary to do so in the present context.

More important, both Georgia and the Cherokees acted because the federal government had not taken a clear position in the dispute. Federal officials neither publicly opposed Georgia's position nor publicly supported the Cherokees. The election of Andrew Jackson as president in 1828 appeared to indicate that the federal government would be more likely to aid Georgia. Indeed, Jackson's push for the Indian Removal Act early in his presidency proved that support. But presidential opinion alone did not necessarily have the power to decide the issue.

Therefore, it became crucial as to how and when the federal government became involved in this struggle between the Cherokee Nation and Georgia. Through its policy based on treaty negotiation, the U.S. government had set two particular standards. First, that the federal government was the primary authority in Indian affairs. Second, that a treaty was an agreement between two sovereign entities. By its actions, the state of Georgia had shown that it would oppose those positions. The Cherokees, on the other hand, placed great importance on the second standard. It remained to be seen what stand the federal government would take.

Cherokees and the Supreme Court

"MARSHALL HAS MADE HIS RULING. NOW LET'S SEE HIM enforce it." For years, scholars, textbooks, and other sources have credited President Andrew Jackson with those words, or at least words similar to those. Jackson allegedly made that declaration when he first heard about Supreme Court Chief Justice John Marshall's ruling in the landmark case of *Worcester v. Georgia* in March 1832. It would be interesting to know whether or not Jackson actually uttered that specific phrase in response to Marshall's decision. However, it is more important to recognize and acknowledge the intentions and ideas lying behind that quotation. In the end, it does not matter if Jackson used that exact phrasing or not. The president's actions in the spring of 1832 and the years that followed proved that he did not intend to enforce the decision of the Supreme Court.

Jackson's position on this issue was extremely important because it played a deciding role in the struggle between the Cherokees and Georgia. *Worcester v. Georgia* was one of two crucial lawsuits heard by the Supreme Court in the early

1830s. Each hearing showcased not only the debate between the state of Georgia and the Cherokee Nation, but also the role of the federal government in that dispute. The first case was dismissed on a legal technicality. The second received the full attention of the court and defined the boundaries of power for states, Indian tribes, and the federal government. Both remained critical turning points in the struggle over Cherokee self-government and Indian removal.

(continues on page 41)

John Ross, or Tsan-usdi, was the son of a Scottish father and a half-Cherokee mother. During the early 1800s, he became one of the leaders of Cherokee resistance to the acquisition of his people's land and would later serve as principal chief of the Cherokees during the 1830s.

WORCESTER V. GEORGIA

On March 3, 1832, the U.S. Supreme Court delivered its decision on the critical case of *Worcester v. Georgia*. Samuel Worcester, a Methodist missionary, had been arrested by Georgia officials for residing on Cherokee lands without obtaining the proper license from the state. He had been sentenced to four years of hard labor but appealed that ruling. The arguments of the case revolved around one critical question: Did Georgia have authority over Cherokee lands within the state's boundaries? If Georgia did, then it had the right both to extend its laws over the Cherokees and arrest Worcester. If Georgia did not, then Worcester was innocent and the state had no authority over the Cherokees and their lands. In a dramatic decision, Marshall and his colleagues ruled in favor of Worcester and against Georgia. The following are selected excerpts from Marshall's written opinion in the case.

This cause, in every point of view in which it can be placed, is of the deepest interest.

The defendant is a State, a member of the Union, which has exercised the powers of government over a people who deny its jurisdiction, and are under the protection of the United States.

The plaintiff is a citizen of the State of Vermont, condemned to hard labor for four years in the penitentiary of Georgia under color of an act which he alleges to be repugnant to the Constitution, laws, and treaties of the United States. . . .

We must inquire and decide whether the act of the Legislature of Georgia under which the plaintiff in error has been persecuted and condemned, be consistent with, or repugnant to the Constitution, laws and treaties of the United States.

It has been said at the bar that the acts of the Legislature of Georgia seize on the whole Cherokee country, parcel it out among

(continues)

(continued)

the neighboring counties of the State, extend her code over the whole country, abolish its institutions and its laws, and annihilate its political existence. . . .

The extraterritorial power of every Legislature being limited in its action to its own citizens or subjects, the very passage of this act is an assertion of jurisdiction over the Cherokee Nation, and of the rights and powers consequent on jurisdiction.

The first step, then, in the inquiry which the Constitution and the laws impose on this court, is an examination of the rightfulness of this claim. . . .

From the commencement of our government Congress has passed acts to regulate trade and intercourse with the Indians; which treat them as nations, respect their rights, and manifest a firm purpose to afford that protection which treaties stipulate. All these acts, and especially that of 1802, which is still in force, manifestly consider the several Indian nations as distinct political communities, having territorial boundaries, within which their authority is exclusive, and having a right to all the lands within those boundaries, which is not only acknowledged, but guaranteed by the United States. . . .

The Cherokee Nation, then, is a distinct community, occupying its own territory, with boundaries accurately described, in which the laws of Georgia can have no force, and which the citizens of Georgia have no right to enter but with the assent of the Cherokees themselves or in conformity with treaties and with the acts of Congress. The whole intercourse between the United States and this nation is, by our Constitution and laws, vested in the government of the United States.

The act of the State of Georgia under which the plaintiff in error was prosecuted is consequently void, and the judgment a nullity. . . . The Acts of Georgia are repugnant to the Constitution, laws, and treaties of the United States.

(continued from page 38)

The existence of these two cases also indicated the intentions of the elected leadership of the Cherokee Nation. John Ross, the principal chief in the 1830s, believed that the Cherokees needed to rely on the U.S. legal system to resist Georgia and removal. He was determined to prove in a court of law that the Cherokees, as an independent nation, did not have to submit to the authority of the state of Georgia. This faith and confidence in the judicial system of the United States resulted in a historical legal victory for the Cherokee Nation. However, Jackson's stance meant that this victory would not move beyond the courtroom.

CHEROKEE NATION V. GEORGIA

Ross knew that the Cherokees could not sit and wait for the federal government to help their cause. Instead, the Cherokees needed to assert and defend their rights. They had written a constitution, elected a government, and proclaimed their sovereignty. Yet these actions had not ended their struggle. On the ground and in the halls of government, they still had to negotiate their sovereignty with Georgia. To counteract the opposition of the state, the Cherokees needed to appeal to the federal government for protection.

In the late 1820s, Cherokee men and women dealt with Georgians on a daily basis. The citizens of Georgia were both eager to obtain more land and aware of their state's position on jurisdiction. Therefore, they did not refrain from crossing into or settling in Cherokee territory. They hoped that the Cherokees would soon remove west of the Mississippi River, and so they claimed land in anticipation of that departure. Some Georgians also entered Cherokee territory to mine gold that had been discovered there in 1828. Though gold finds occurred on non-Indian lands as well, miners and fortune hunters refused to respect the Cherokee Nation's borders. Frequent conflicts resulted, but these Georgians had the full support of their state government. Indeed, when Georgia extended its laws over the Cherokees in 1829, it included a provision to protect the mines and miners located on Indian lands.

To make matters worse, Georgia officials continued to pass laws and allow behavior that encouraged Indian removal and undermined the Cherokees' way of life. The Georgia Guard, a volunteer militia organized under state law, used threats and violence against the Cherokees. Meanwhile, the Georgia legislature enacted a law making it illegal to prevent any Indian from choosing to remove. This act specifically targeted the Christian missionaries among the Cherokees who supported the Indians in their fight against Georgia's policies.

When it came to fulfilling the territorial needs of its citizens, Georgia officials acted without regard to Cherokee claims. Indeed, the state hoped that offering Indian lands to its citizens through a lottery would further undermine Cherokee resistance to removal. Some Georgians used other strategies to pressure the Cherokees. Elias Boudinot, editor of the *Cherokee Phoenix*, reported in July 1829 on the efforts of some of the state's newspapers: "The eagerness which is manifested in Geo. to obtain the lands of the Cherokees has frequently led the journals of that state to deceive the people by stating that we [the Cherokees] are 'making extensive preparations to remove to the west.'"[6] Boudinot was quick to assure anyone reading his editorial that no such preparations were underway.

Nevertheless, the continued harassment brought forth by Georgia's laws, along with the persistent intrusions of settlers and miners, made it extremely difficult for the Cherokees to resist in a peaceful manner. And Congress's debate over and its vote in favor of the Indian Removal Act in May 1830 was the final step that pushed the Cherokees into action. Despite the impassioned speeches of those who opposed the bill, the ultimate success of that legislation reinforced the conclusion that the Indians did not have the support of Congress or the president. From the perspective of Ross and other members of the Cherokee government, their best hope lay in bringing their argument to the courtroom, where a legal victory might overcome the interests of state and federal governments.

The Cherokees' decision to resist removal by legal means received support from a number of sources in U.S. society. In 1829, without any request from the Cherokees, an attorney named Jeremiah Evarts wrote a brief that attacked the idea of removal. Titled *Essays on the Present Crisis*, this document examined the historical relationship between the United States and the Cherokee Nation. Based on this history, Evarts concluded first that the Cherokees had sole authority over their land, and second, that the federal government, not Georgia, should have authority in Indian affairs. Although Evarts did not become the attorney in the proceedings that followed, his writings influenced how the Cherokees presented their argument. Instead of Evarts, though, Ross and the Cherokees hired William Wirt to argue their case before the Supreme Court. Wirt, an easterner in his late 50s, had served as U.S. attorney general for 12 years. He was an experienced attorney who had appeared numerous times before the court. Although he was initially reluctant to participate in a case that challenged President Jackson, Wirt accepted the Cherokees' offer.

Wirt was hired as the attorney, but Ross and the Cherokees did not stay quiet during the preparations for trial. They had hired Wirt because at the time no Cherokee had the legal training necessary to argue in front of the Supreme Court. Ross and the Cherokee National Council also wanted to make sure that Wirt addressed all of the relevant legal questions. They sent letters to him asking for a summary of his opinions on the legal issues at stake. Ross also consulted with Evarts over the possibility of hiring another lawyer to help in the case. Over a period of several months, the Cherokees, Wirt, and their supporters worked together to prepare for their day in court.

In 1830, John Ross and a delegation of Cherokees selected former U.S. attorney general William Wirt to represent them in their case against the state of Georgia. Wirt argued that the Cherokees constituted a foreign nation and thus were not subject to U.S. law.

With this input from the Cherokee leadership and the ideas presented in Evarts's document, Wirt constructed the case around a single premise. The Cherokees were a nation. This principle served as the linchpin for the argument put forth by Wirt and the Cherokees. To present their brief to the court in 1830, therefore, Wirt and the Cherokees filed as a foreign nation. Use of this status allowed the Cherokees to invoke the authority of the Supreme Court under Article III of the U.S. Constitution. According to the argument proposed by Wirt and his clients, Georgia's state laws were unconstitutional and had no standing because of the Cherokees' status. Those laws undermined the Cherokees' position as an independent nation. Just as important, the Georgia legislation contradicted the laws and treaties of the U.S. government.

Governor Wilson Lumpkin and the state of Georgia not only refused to acknowledge the Cherokee position but also opposed the authority of the Supreme Court. Lumpkin expected the Cherokees to give up their legal battle and move west of the Mississippi River. Georgia also held true to the stance it had first assumed in the 1790s. The state continued to oppose the notion that the U.S. Supreme Court had the authority to rule on state laws. In fact, attorneys for Georgia never even showed up in court to present an oral argument.

The final decision announced in the spring of 1831 focused on the actual status of the Cherokee Nation. Specifically, it ruled on the Cherokees' strategy to file as a foreign nation. Chief Justice Marshall wrote the opinion. In that statement, the court did not even address the Cherokees' challenge against the authority of Georgia's laws. Nor did the court make a declaration favoring Georgia. Instead, Marshall and his colleagues concluded that the Supreme Court would not decide the facts of the case because the Cherokees were not a foreign nation.

Rather than make a ruling, the Supreme Court dismissed the Cherokees' case on this technicality. To help explain the decision, Marshall created a term that has remained important and has been debated to the present day. Neither the Cherokee nor any Indian tribe could be considered a foreign nation. Instead, Marshall stated, the Cherokee tribe should be described as a "domestic dependent nation." The chief justice based this conclusion in part on principles of land ownership. Because the Cherokees only had a right of occupancy, they did not exist as an independent nation. The

U.S. government, as the true owner of the land, was a guardian for all Indian tribes, including the Cherokee. Therefore, the Cherokees' residence within the borders of the United States made them domestic. Their status as wards of the federal government made them dependent. But although their race and culture made them nationally distinct from the United States, it did not make them an independent foreign nation.

Chief Ross, however, refused to allow Marshall's ruling to undermine the Cherokees' determination to fight this battle in court. He recognized that the decision was not necessarily the defeat that it may have appeared at first. "I sincerely believe," Ross declared in an April 14 speech to the Cherokees, "that a foundation is laid upon which our injured rights may be reared & made permanent."[7] The Cherokee leader had wanted a legal victory, so in that regard the ruling was a disappointment. Yet from his perspective, the Cherokees had suffered a temporary setback rather than a loss.

This Supreme Court decision had two related consequences. It allowed Marshall and his colleagues to avoid ruling on a divisive issue. Neither Georgia nor President Jackson wanted the court to rule in favor of the Cherokees. However, the conclusions presented in *Cherokee Nation v. Georgia* also did nothing to end the controversy. To argue that the Cherokee tribe was not a foreign nation, the court had to ignore the numerous treaties signed between the Indians and the U.S. government during the previous decades. More important, the opinions presented by the justices never concluded that state laws should have authority over Indians. As Ross had concluded, the door remained open for another case.

WORCESTER V. GEORGIA

The next opportunity for the Cherokees to contest Georgia's authority arose shortly after the 1831 decision. On July 15 of that year, Georgia officials arrested two men—Reverend Samuel Austin Worcester and Reverend Elihu Butler. The two Protestant missionaries had broken one of the laws passed by the state legislature to extend Georgia's authority. This particular law required all white men to obtain a license from the state to reside within the boundaries of the Cherokee Nation. More than an expression of state power, the regulation targeted those individuals, especially teachers and missionaries, who supported the Cherokees and their fight against removal. Worcester and Butler and their missionary efforts qualified. Their trial took place two months after their arrest and both men were found guilty. The judge sentenced each man to four years of hard labor.

This arrest did not happen by chance. Worcester was a missionary from Vermont who worked in the Cherokee Nation under the auspices of the American Board of Commissioners for Foreign Missions. He first arrived in the region during the 1810s and helped Elias Boudinot establish the *Cherokee Phoenix*. More to the point, Worcester opposed the extension of Georgia's laws and supported the right of the Cherokees to govern the lives of their people. The missionary believed that his arrest would allow the Cherokees to successfully contest Georgia's laws. He also hoped that the arrest of a Christian missionary, a figure whom many sympathized with, would raise opposition to Georgia and Indian removal throughout the country.

Worcester's seizure and imprisonment brought the dispute between Georgia and the Cherokees to the U.S. Supreme Court for the second time in as many years. Unlike *Cherokee Nation v. Georgia*, this case could not be dismissed on a technicality. As a white man and a U.S. citizen, Worcester had firm legal standing in court. Marshall and his colleagues would have to decide whether or not Georgia had the right to extend its laws over the Cherokee Nation.

The hearings began in February 1832, and the two sides presented arguments consistent with positions taken in the past. The attorneys for Worcester and Butler made their case simple. They argued that Georgia did not have the right to extend its laws into a realm reserved for the federal government. According to the U.S. Constitution and based on congressional legislation of decades past, only U.S. officials and Congress had authority in Indian affairs. The missionaries' attorneys also argued that the Cherokees represented a nation with "powers of self-government." Georgia once more refused to send any representatives to make oral arguments. The state remained steadfast and did not budge from its stand challenging the authority of the Supreme Court.

On the third day of March, the Supreme Court presented its decision. Marshall and his colleagues ruled in favor of the missionaries and against the state of Georgia. The court declared that all state legislation targeting the Cherokees was unconstitutional. Instead of avoiding the issue, as had happened in the 1831 dismissal, this time the court made its position very clear. The Georgia laws, wrote Marshall, were "repugnant to the constitution, laws, and treaties of the United States." Three of the remaining six justices agreed that Georgia's actions had defied the authority of the federal government.

More important, those same justices agreed that the laws had violated the political authority of the Cherokee Nation. Although the case revolved around the missionaries and Georgia, Marshall used the opportunity to present the court's conclusions on Indian sovereignty. One central issue that remained was over ownership of the land. In this matter, the Supreme Court had to negotiate all of its past judgments on the doctrine of discovery and the right of occupancy. Marshall used the 1832 ruling to emphasize that regardless of any past decisions, Indian lands could only be obtained through consent. The U.S. government did not have the right or the authority to seize Indian lands without proper negotiations.

On March 3, 1832, Chief Justice John Marshall handed down the decision in *Worcester v. Georgia*, which upheld the fact that the Cherokees did indeed comprise a sovereign nation and that the citizens of Georgia had no right to enter their territory.

Marshall also attempted to refine the terms used in his 1831 written statement. He still argued that the Cherokees did not have standing as a foreign nation. However, he stressed the fact that prior treaties with the Cherokees recognized the Indians' right to self-government. From a legal perspective, the relationship between the Cherokees and the United States had also acknowledged the national character of the Cherokee political structure. Even the definition of the guardian-ward relationship did not undermine this status. "A weak state," Marshall wrote in reference to the Cherokee Nation, "in order to provide for its safety, may place itself under the protection of one more powerful, without stripping itself of the right of government, and ceasing to be a state."[8] Marshall and the court did not back off completely from their 1831 decision. However, their ruling in *Worcester v. Georgia* did provide more support for the Cherokees' status as a nation.

The 1832 decision was a significant legal victory for the Cherokees. Coming less than a year after the disappointment of *Cherokee Nation v. Georgia*, this decision gave hope to Ross and his people. Boudinot told his older brother Stand Watie: "The question is for ever settled as to who is right and who is wrong, and the controversy is exactly where it ought to be, and where we have all along been desirous it should be."[9] By denouncing the Georgia laws in such blatant terms, the Supreme Court had proclaimed that the federal government should support the Cherokees and end Georgia's harassment.

Two circumstances sabotaged this triumph. First, Governor Lumpkin of Georgia refused to recognize the authority of the Supreme Court and did not release the prisoners. Second, the nature of the federal government allowed President Jackson to undermine the court's decision by doing nothing. The checks and balances created by the U.S. Constitution do not allow the judicial branch to enforce its rulings. Instead, enforcement rests in the hands of the president and the executive branch. President Andrew Jackson had no intention of following through on Marshall's decision. As a result, the Cherokees' legal victory would stay in the courtroom.

CONCLUSION

Jackson ignored the Supreme Court for two particular reasons. First and foremost, he had long supported Indian removal and believed that the Cherokees would be much better off if they simply joined their relatives west of the Mississippi River. By not enforcing the 1832 decision, he made that removal much more likely. Second, the Supreme Court rendered its decision during a period of increased tension over states' rights. President Jackson was already at odds with South Carolina over economic issues like the tariff. Even if he had supported the Cherokee cause, he believed that he could not afford to offend Georgia.

The 1832 ruling and the lack of enforcement left Ross and the Cherokees with several crucial decisions to make. Their legal strategy had worked remarkably well and they had achieved the victory for which they had exerted so much time and effort. Yet, due to the reactions of Georgia and Jackson, all of that hard work was for naught. Georgia's refusal to recognize the authority of the Supreme Court emboldened its citizens. Incidents of trespass and violence on Cherokee lands increased in the early 1830s. Meanwhile, Jackson's refusal to enforce the decision struck a blow at the morale of the Cherokee Nation as a whole. Despite all of their efforts and their faith in the U.S. legal system, the lawsuits had left them no better off than when they began. Now they needed to decide if they should continue to use the same approach or if they needed a new one.

The Treaty of New Echota and the Aftermath

IN AUGUST 1837, ELIAS BOUDINOT EXPRESSED HIS opinion regarding his tribe's future: "Removal, then, is the only remedy—the only *practicable* remedy. By it there *may be* finally a renovation—our people *may* rise from their very ashes to become prosperous and happy, and a credit to our race. Such has been and is now my opinion, and under such a settled opinion I have acted in this affair."[10] Boudinot wrote that statement less than two years after he and 20 other Cherokee men signed the Treaty of New Echota. Under the terms of that accord, the Cherokees ceded all of their lands east of the Mississippi River. They further agreed to relocate to new homes in the western territories within two years. In the above statement and others, Boudinot explained his reasons for consenting to that agreement and defended his signature on the treaty. He firmly believed that he had made the right choice and had acted to save his people.

Boudinot had to defend his decision. The treaty negotiated at the town of New Echota in December 1835 was a controversial agreement that created serious divisions within the

Andrew Jackson, the seventh president of the United States, was an advocate of Indian removal and negotiated several treaties that forced southern tribes to give up their land to the United States. Consequently, it did not come as a surprise when Jackson supported Georgians' rights to settle on Cherokee land after the Supreme Court handed down the *Worcester v. Georgia* decision.

Cherokee Nation. Boudinot and the other members of what became known as the Treaty Party had acted on their beliefs. Those actions went against the sentiments of the majority of the Cherokee Nation and broke Cherokee law. Ross and other members of the Cherokee government condemned the treaty and asked Congress to reject its provisions. Their protest failed and the U.S. Senate ratified the treaty on May 18, 1836.

The Treaty of New Echota can be seen as both a cause and an effect. As a cause, its ratification ended the legal battles of the previous years. Despite the protests and arguments of Ross and others, the U.S. government now had a ratified document that could be used to justify and enforce the removal of the Cherokees from their lands in the Southeast. The treaty was also an effect. Boudinot and the Treaty Party signed the agreement because they did not think the Cherokees could remain on their lands. President Jackson's decision to ignore *Worcester v. Georgia* had confirmed their beliefs that the people of the United States would not support the Cherokees. According to Boudinot and the other members of the Treaty Party, only through removal would the Cherokees survive.

BOUDINOT AND THE TREATY PARTY

In the late 1820s and early 1830s, as the citizens of Georgia pushed for removal, members of the Cherokee Nation presented their opinions on the matter in the pages of the *Cherokee Phoenix.* A group of Cherokee women submitted a petition to the paper in October 1831 and argued against relocation. "And we sincerely hope," they declared, "there is no consideration which can induce our citizens to forsake the land of our fathers of which they have been in possession from time immemorial, and thus compel us, against our will, to undergo the toils and difficulties of removing with our helpless families hundreds of miles to unhealthy and unproductive country."[11] There had been debates within the Cherokee Nation about removal before. Yet most of those who had favored relocation in the first two decades of the 1800s had already moved to Arkansas Territory. Only when President Jackson chose to ignore the Supreme Court did a segment of the Cherokee Nation east of the Mississippi River begin to consider emigration a good idea.

The very editor who chose to print the Cherokee women's petition was one of the most prominent Cherokees to speak out in favor of relocation. Boudinot did not come to his decision lightly to support removal. He had been an opponent of removal and an advocate of Cherokee assimilation for many years. As a product of several missionary schools and the original editor of the *Cherokee Phoenix*, Boudinot was a perfect example of the Cherokees' efforts to change the nature of their society. Like the other members of the Treaty Party, he also believed that the Cherokees' attempts at negotiation had been undermined once and for all by the actions of Georgia and President Jackson. From his perspective, removal was the only and best option for the survival of the Cherokee Nation.

Boudinot's birth name was Gallegina, though as a child he went by Buck. He was born in 1804 in the settlement of Oothcaloga, in presenet-day northwestern Georgia. His father, Oo-watie, and mother, Susanna Reese, lived on an individual homestead and fenced their fields. This lifestyle differed from those traditional Cherokee settlements centered on villages. Boudinot's parents supported Cherokee efforts to adopt the ways of white culture and enrolled Buck, their eldest son, in a local Moravian mission school when he was seven years old. In 1817, with the consent of his parents, Buck traveled north with a Protestant missionary and enrolled at a school in Cornwall, Connecticut. The 13-year-old changed his name to that of a white man who financially supported his schooling, thus enrolling under the name of Elias Boudinot.

The years at Cornwall changed Boudinot's life in many ways. He not only furthered his education but also converted to Christianity. In addition, he met the young woman whom he later married in 1826. Harriet Gold was a white woman and the daughter of a local physician. At the announcement of their engagement, local citizens of Cornwall gathered on the town green and burned the couple in effigy. Their outrage over the union of the interracial couple made Boudinot rethink his ideas about civilization. In particular, he began to doubt whether white Americans would ever accept Cherokees or any Indians regardless of the Indians' efforts to change their ways of life.

In 1827, the Cherokee government offered Boudinot the position of editor for the *Cherokee Phoenix*, the first newspaper published by and for the Cherokee Nation. The *Phoenix* published in English and Cherokee and included official correspondence and legislation, wedding notices, and meeting times for temperance societies and other organizations. Boudinot also took advantage of the readership beyond the Cherokee Nation. He promoted Cherokee society and showed the United States and its citizens that the Cherokees had made advancements in civilization and would benefit from avoiding removal. Through the paper, Boudinot made every effort to refute outside assumptions about Cherokee savagery, poverty, and uncivilized ways.

Both his viewpoints and his position in the Cherokee Nation changed in 1832. Boudinot, like all Cherokees, rejoiced over Chief Justice Marshall's decision in *Worcester v. Georgia*. He was just as upset over Jackson's refusal to enforce that ruling. In his mind, this inaction meant a final defeat. For Boudinot, the only hope for Cherokee survival now rested in removal to the West. He signed a petition circulated by some Cherokees that supported this conclusion. As editor of the *Phoenix*, he also believed the paper could serve as a place to voice his opinions. Ross and the Cherokee government disagreed. In August 1832, they made Boudinot resign his position as editor, with Ross justifying the decision in a note to the Cherokees' General Council. "The toleration of *diversified views* to the columns of such a paper," he explained, "would not fail to create fermentation and confusion among our citizens, and in the end prove injurious to the welfare of the nation."[12] Ross and other leaders refused to allow the paper to express any views in support of removal.

Other Cherokees shared Boudinot's beliefs that removal was the best available option. Foremost among those men were two of his relatives. Major Ridge was Oo-watie's brother, and therefore Boudinot's uncle. John Ridge, Major's son, was Boudinot's cousin and had also attended the school in Cornwall. The Ridges had shared in the joy over *Worcester v. Georgia* and the dismay over Jackson's decisions. They also took notice of the men hired by the state of Georgia to survey the Cherokee territory for white settlers. And they listened when members of Congress who once opposed removal said that they could no longer protect Cherokee lands.

From the autumn of 1832 to the winter of 1835, John and Major Ridge debated the issue of removal with Ross and his followers. They did not think Ross was acting in the best interests of the nation. Ross traveled to Washington, D.C., in the spring of 1833 to discuss the Cherokees' circumstances with U.S. officials. In one meeting, President Jackson offered $3 million for the Cherokee lands east of the Mississippi River. Ross refused. He knew that the western Cherokees had signed a treaty in 1828 that relocated them from lands in Arkansas Territory that had been given to them only decades earlier. Based on those events, Ross refused to believe Jackson's assurances that Cherokee lands in the West would be protected from white settlers.

John and Major Ridge were not pleased that Ross had been so quick to reject Jackson's offer. Both men were elected members of the Cherokee government and spoke openly in council about their support for a removal treaty. However, the overwhelming majority of Cherokee officials backed Ross. And while most Cherokees refused to listen to the Ridges, the

Cherokee government took action against the two men. In August 1833, the Cherokee National Council removed the Ridges from office for "maintaining opinions and a policy to terminate the existence of the Cherokee community on the

MAJOR RIDGE AND JOHN ROSS: PROMINENT CHEROKEE LEADERS

Major Ridge was born around 1771 in the town of Hiwasee in what is now eastern Tennessee. His mother was of Scottish and Cherokee descent and his father was a Cherokee man noted for his hunting prowess. His brother, Oo-watie, was the father of Elias Boudinot and Stand Watie. The Cherokee name he earned in his youth was Kahmungdaclageh, or "the man who walks on the mountaintop." This loosely translated to The Ridge, and he gained the title of Major after his military service against the Creek Indians between 1813 and 1814.

By the late 1790s, Ridge lived at the Pine Log settlement in northern Georgia and represented this town at the Cherokee tribal council. Known for his oratorical skills, Ridge was the driving force behind the council's decision at the end of the decade to change the Cherokees' traditional code of vengeance that called for retribution in murder cases. Ridge also devoted his efforts to building a home with his wife, Susanna, raising livestock, and farming the land. Like other Cherokees of his economic status, he relied on African-American slaves to perform most of the labor on his farm. By the 1820s, Ridge was both a wealthy planter and a prominent member of the Cherokee National Council. In 1829, he successfully advocated for the passage of a law that decreed the death penalty for any Cherokee who illegally sold tribal land. He subsequently broke this law by signing the Treaty of New Echota in 1835 and was killed in June 1839.

lands of [their] fathers."[13] Promotion of removal would not be tolerated.

The dismissal of the Ridges from office and the widespread support for Ross did not end the debate. Although the majority of Cherokee voters had elected Ross to the office of

John Ross was born in 1790, the son of a Scottish trader named Daniel Ross and a Scottish-Cherokee woman named Molly McDonald. His heritage made him one-eighth Cherokee, a fact often used by U.S. officials to attack his Indian identity. But among the Cherokees, his mother's status bestowed membership in the Bird Clan to him. Daniel Ross made sure that all of his children received an education, and so John attended at least three different schools in his youth. At the age of 24, he served with the Cherokee forces at the Battle of Horseshoe Bend and a year later opened a trading store on the Tennessee River.

Along with his merchant business at the place soon known as Ross's Landing (near present-day Chattanooga, Tennessee), the Cherokee trader owned a sizeable farm worked primarily by slaves. Ross supported the adoption of the practices of U.S. society and encouraged the establishment of missionary schools among the Cherokees. He also became an active participant in the Cherokee government. Ross served as president of the National Committee from 1819 to 1826 and was a primary author of the Cherokee Constitution, adopted in 1827. The Cherokees elected Ross as principal chief in October 1828. Because of his heritage and his appearance, many U.S. officials and citizens accused Ross of not being a true Indian. Ross, however, was Cherokee through his mother and his opponents within the Cherokee Nation never attacked his credentials as a member of the community. He led the Cherokee Nation according to the will of the people and maintained a tremendous amount of influence among the Cherokees, serving as their principal chief until his death in 1866.

Major Ridge, whose first name came from his military rank during the Creek War of 1813–14, was a wealthy planter and prominent member of the Cherokee National Council. Despite being an advocate of the death penalty for any Cherokee who illegally sold tribal land, Ridge broke this law by signing the Treaty of New Echota in 1835.

principal chief, he also had a number of detractors inside and outside of the Cherokee Nation. His Cherokee opponents argued that Ross was leading the Cherokees astray by convincing them that their land could still be saved. They accused Ross of manipulating the minds of the less educated among the Cherokees. Outsiders made similar accusations. They also added an additional charge. Because Ross was only one-eighth Cherokee by birth, they argued that he was not really an Indian and that he had convinced the Cherokees to resist removal solely for his own economic and political gain. Such accusations ignored the fact that regardless of fractions of his heritage, Ross was a Cherokee by descent from his mother.

During the course of 1835, both the Ridges and Ross maintained separate communications with U.S. officials and held councils with the Cherokee people. The position of the Cherokee Nation was clear. The overwhelming majority of

Like his father, Major, John Ridge was a signatory of the 1835 Treaty of New Echota and supported Cherokee removal. As part of the treaty, the Cherokees agreed to cede all their land east of the Mississippi River to the U.S. government and move west within two years.

Cherokees opposed the notion of removal. Ross did his best both to disrupt the efforts of the Ridges and to push the United States to richly compensate the Cherokees for their lands. At one point, Ross proposed that the Cherokees would remove if the United States paid them $20 million. The federal government quickly rejected this price as far too high. For the most part, officials paid more attention to the Ridges and their allies. As the federal government continued to push for a treaty, the Ridges and Boudinot gained an upper hand because of their support for such an accord.

Commissioner John F. Schermerhorn negotiated a tentative treaty with the Ridges and their allies in March 1835. The terms included a payment of $5 million for Cherokee lands in the East. Now the Cherokee people had to be convinced that such a deal made sense. Though the Ridges attempted to sell the benefits of the treaty in the months that followed, Ross and his supporters did everything in their power to battle against it. The men who favored the treaty may have had an advantage in Washington, but Ross was able to work against them very effectively among the Cherokees.

Then, late in 1835, when Ross traveled to Washington with a Cherokee delegation to discuss the terms of this possible agreement, Schermerhorn finalized the Treaty of New Echota back in Georgia. The Cherokee delegation left in early December and included Ross, John Ridge, and Stand Watie. Only a few weeks after the departure of that delegation, Schermerhorn held a council at the former Cherokee capital of New Echota. Fewer than 400 Cherokees joined him. Both Boudinot and Major Ridge addressed those in attendance and urged them to agree to remove. "We cannot remain here in safety and comfort," Major Ridge advised the Cherokees. "I would willingly die to preserve them [Cherokee lands], but any forcible effort to keep them will cost us our lands, our lives, and the lives of our children."[14] On December 29, a committee of 20 men sat down with Schermerhorn and signed the treaty.

With the signatures and marks of those 20 men, the deed was done. Under this agreement, the Cherokees ceded all of their land east of the Mississippi River and agreed to move west within two years. Ross received word of the treaty while he and the Cherokee delegation were still in Washington. John Ridge and Stand Watie both signed a copy of the treaty while they were still in the city. Everyone involved recognized the gravity of their actions. Major Ridge understood clearly what he had done. In a statement to Colonel Thomas McKenney, the Cherokee leader remarked of his signature, "I expect to die for it."[15]

The Treaty of New Echota marked the beginning of two new chapters for the Cherokee Nation. First, it signaled the birth of the Treaty Party. From that point forward, the Ridges, Elias Boudinot, and others would be associated with that document. Their names would be forever linked to the cession of all Cherokee lands east of the Mississippi River. The treaty negotiation also set in motion one more battle for Chief Ross and the Cherokee Nation. Faced with yet another critical setback, they now lobbied Congress to reject what they argued was a fraudulent treaty.

TREATY RATIFICATION AND CHEROKEE PROTESTS

Most Cherokees believed that the 1835 treaty was invalid. Because the Ridges had been removed from office, they and the other men who signed the document did not have any right to cede land. Indeed, their decision to negotiate and sign the treaty without the proper authority broke a law passed by the Cherokee government in 1829. And according to law, the penalty for their action was death. However, the ultimate question was not whether the Cherokees believed in the treaty. Ross and the Cherokee Nation had to convince the U.S. Congress to reject it.

Speeches in both houses of Congress in 1835 and 1836 revealed some continued opposition to removal. Although only the Senate had authority over treaty ratification, members of the House of Representatives took to the floor to express their outrage. The treaty was an "eternal disgrace upon the country," according to former president and current representative John Quincy Adams. Many senators, including Henry Clay and Daniel Webster, even assured Ross that the treaty would not be ratified.

In the end, the determination of President Jackson and the efforts of just enough senators would overcome the opposition and outcry. Approaching the end of his second term and determined to secure the removal of the Cherokees, Jackson used all of his influence to gain ratification of the treaty. (The Senate voted to ratify by only one vote.) Despite the efforts of its opponents, the Treaty of New Echota became law on May 23, 1836.

Ross continued to protest the treaty even after the Senate vote. He refused to consent to the validity of the document and pressed the U.S. government to undo what had been done. Despite the protests, in the two years after the final vote in Congress, the U.S. government proceeded with plans for the removal of the Cherokees.

REMOVAL AND ROUNDUP

In the summer of 1836, members of the Treaty Party, along with their families and followers, prepared to move west. According to the treaty, the U.S. government would pay the expenses of removal and would also provide provisions for one year after the journey. Not all Cherokees who consented to removal made the journey at the same time.

The first emigrant party encompassed nearly 600 Cherokees and left for western lands at the beginning of 1837. These

Cherokee men, women, and children, accompanied by their slaves, horses, oxen, and other material possessions, made the journey via land. Their route took them through Tennessee, Kentucky, Illinois, Missouri, and Arkansas Territory. Major Ridge and his family left with about 500 Cherokees on March 3 of the same year. John Ridge, Elias Boudinot, and their families began their emigration in June as part of a much smaller contingent. They settled in present-day northeastern Oklahoma, among the Cherokees who had moved west decades earlier.

May 23, 1838, marked the deadline for Cherokee removal as established by the 1835 treaty. By that date, nearly 2,000 Cherokees had moved west under the terms of the accord. That number was far below the federal government's hopes and expectations, and approximately 16,000 Cherokees remained on their lands east of the Mississippi River.

U.S. officials set plans in motion to round up those Cherokees who continued to resist the treaty. The approach depended on the use of military force, and General George Winfield Scott arrived in Cherokee Territory in early May to oversee the removal. He first addressed the Cherokee Nation together and urged them to prepare to be moved. Next, he told his army of nearly 7,000 regulars and volunteers to perform their duties in a humane fashion.

During the following several weeks and months, the soldiers under Scott's command collected the Cherokees and placed them in internment camps until the actual removal could be arranged. Despite Scott's statements to his troops, the process was brutal. The Cherokees were given no time to gather their belongings before they were seized and taken from their homes. Most belongings were left behind. Depending on where they were when the soldiers found them, men, women, and children were either taken with or separated from their families.

As fall approached in 1838, the conditions of the Cherokees residing east and west of the Mississippi River presented

In May 1838, General George Winfield Scott arrived in Cherokee territory to oversee the removal of the tribe. Over the following months, Scott and his "Army of the Cherokee Nation" rounded up thousands of Cherokees for the trip west.

opposing pictures. Elias Boudinot, the Ridges, and other members of the Treaty Party were recovering from the relocation. Not all of their journeys had been easy, and sickness had plagued some of the emigrant parties. Now they prepared to establish a new home in the West. At the same time, the Cherokees in Georgia stood behind stockade fences under the eyes and guns of U.S. soldiers. They were prisoners, powerless to prevent settlers from taking over their homes and their lands.

CONCLUSION

The Treaty of New Echota marks the decisive moment in the Cherokees' struggle against removal. When Congress ratified the treaty, the Cherokee Nation finally lost the battle they had waged for years. The federal government now had a legal document that granted it the rights to Cherokee lands. The vision shared by Jackson and many others in the United States would be realized.

The treaty was and is highly controversial. Boudinot, the Ridges, and the remaining members of the Treaty Party believed that they acted in the best interests of the Cherokee people. Ross and the majority of the Cherokee Nation disagreed. The Treaty Party did not have any authority to cede the lands east of the Mississippi River and by signing the treaty they therefore broke Cherokee law. Instead of recognizing those facts, a narrow majority of the U.S. Senate chose to overlook them. And the U.S. soldiers arrived in the late spring of 1838 to enforce their decision.

On the
Trail of Tears

ROSS AND THE CHEROKEE COUNCIL CONTINUED TO protest the validity of the Treaty of New Echota. However, these leaders realized that they could not prevent the forced removal of their people from the lands east of the Mississippi River. As of May 1838, the Cherokees were at the mercy of General Scott and the soldiers under his command.

The presence of the U.S. soldiers changed the questions faced by the Cherokees. No longer could they debate if removal would occur. Instead, Ross and the Cherokee Council now dealt with when and how it would take place. They were especially concerned with Scott's plan to move their people from the stockades to their new homes in the western territories. To the extent that it was possible, the Cherokee leaders wanted to ensure a safe journey for the thousands of men, women, and children. They knew that relocation would be tough on everyone, whether young or old, healthy or sick. Nearly 900 miles lay between their old homes in Georgia, Tennessee, and Alabama and their new ones in the West. Whether traveling by water or on land, the journey would be

Known as *Nunna daul Tsunyi*, or the "trail where they cried," the forced removal of the Cherokees is engrained in the tribe's identity. During the more than 1,000-mile-long march, approximately 2,000 Cherokees died on their way to Indian Territory (present-day Oklahoma).

difficult. And depending on the time of year, weather conditions could potentially make it worse.

Between June 1838 and March 1839, about 16,000 Cherokees left their eastern lands under the terms of the Treaty of New Echota and arrived at their new homes in the West. The Cherokees referred to the journey as *Nunna daul Tsunyi*, or the "trail where they cried." In most history textbooks, it is known as the Trail of Tears. But it was not a single route. Instead, at least 16 different detachments left the former Cherokee lands between June 6 and December 5, 1838. They arrived at their destination between June 20, 1838, and March

25, 1839. Disease and bad weather conditions haunted the different detachments as they traveled. Hundreds escaped at different points along the journey. Thousands died and were buried along the trail. And though descriptions of the experience remain, words alone will never truly capture the emotional and physical crisis of this event in the history of the Cherokee Nation.

JOHN ROSS AND THE ORGANIZATION OF REMOVAL

In July 1838, the Cherokee leadership wanted to obtain government permission to organize and control the manner in which the removal occurred. On the one hand, they acknowledged that resistance was no longer possible. On the other hand, they took action because of two particular circumstances: The condition of the Cherokees imprisoned in the stockades was deteriorating quickly, and the three detachments forced west by the government between May and July had created fear among the remaining Cherokees. Ross and the Cherokee leadership believed that they had to control the removal process to keep their people safe.

The roundup of Cherokees had taken place during the course of 25 days from May into June. Yet the organization of removal detachments took time, and by early July most Cherokees remained imprisoned in the wooden stockades built along the Georgia-Tennessee border. Most had arrived with only the clothes on their backs and they subsisted on rations supplied by the U.S. government. The cramped living quarters, the unfamiliar food, and the rising temperatures as summer approached made the conditions unbearable. A drought that hit in June further worsened the health of the Cherokees. Dysentery, measles, and whooping cough were only some of the diseases that appeared in the prisons. Before the removal process even began, an estimated 2,000 to 4,000 Cherokees died in those stockades.

Not all of the Cherokees remained imprisoned in the two months before the Cherokee Council asked Congress for permission to control the removal of their people. Three different detachments organized by Scott left for the western territories between June 6 and June 17. The approximate numbers of Cherokees in each party upon departure were 800, 900, and 1,100. Each detachment completed all or most of the journey on flatboats towed behind steamboats.

Together these first three removals indicated future problems and created fears among the Cherokees left behind. Out of the first detachment of 800, fewer than 500 arrived in the West. Most if not all of those missing Cherokees had deserted during the course of the journey. Reports on the two detachments that followed indicated that about 240 Cherokees had died along the way. Each of these parties had traveled during the hot summer months, and the trip had taken its toll.

Captain G. S. Drane led the last detachment, which traveled by water. This party of more than 1,000 Cherokees made their way by wagon train from Ross's Landing on the Tennessee River (at the Georgia-Tennessee border) to Waterloo, Alabama. They then alternated between boat and land travel until their arrival in the West in early September. Drane's report on the removal, though not very descriptive, provides some important insights into the minds of the Cherokees and those who led the removal. Only a week into the journey, more than 200 Cherokees left the detachment and headed back east. "The feelings of discontent among the Emigrants were so great," Drane noted in response to this desertion, "that Genl N. Smith thought it advisable to accept the services of the volunteers as a guard to accompany the Indians to Waterloo, Alabama."[16] Meanwhile, Drane mentioned the 146 deaths on the journey only in a statistical report at the end of his letter.

Drane's report paid more attention to the high number of Cherokees who deserted the removal detachments.

Through these people and through other means, the Cherokees still imprisoned back east heard a number of horror stories about the journey. Tales of drowning and other water dangers made their way through the stockades. It did not help that almost a year earlier, more than 300 members of a Creek Indian removal detachment died when the *Monmouth*, the steamboat on which they were traveling, crashed into another vessel. Overall, the reality of removal and the dangers of water travel created a great deal of

JAMES MOONEY RECOUNTS THE STORY OF TSALI

Ethnologist James Mooney lived among the Eastern Cherokees from 1887 to 1890 and recorded many of the stories and traditions of that community. One of those stories spoke of Tsali, an older Cherokee man executed for violently resisting removal. Tsali and three male relatives were killed for their role in the deaths of two U.S. soldiers in November 1838. There is some dispute over the sequence of events that led to the deaths of those soldiers. Cherokee accounts refer to the harsh force used by the soldiers, while the military reports describe the incident as a surprise attack by Cherokee warriors. The account given below is from Wasitu'na, or Washington, Tsali's youngest son. Washington was not executed in 1838 because of his young age.

One old man named Tsali, "Charley," was seized with his wife, brother, his three sons and their families. Exasperated at the brutality accorded his wife, who, being unable to travel fast, was prodded by bayonets to hasten her steps, he urged the other men to join with him in a dash for liberty. As he spoke in Cherokee the soldiers, although they heard, understood nothing until each warrior suddenly anxiety, and most Cherokees subsequently refused to consider removing by steamboat.

Both the health conditions in the stockades and doubts about the journey itself led Ross and the Cherokee Council to take action. As the temperatures rose with the onset of the northern Georgia summer, General Scott halted the organization of removal detachments. This lull in government action created the opportunity for the Cherokee leadership to make their proposal. Scott approved of their plan, as long

sprang upon the one nearest and endeavored to wrench his gun from him. The attack was so sudden and unexpected that one soldier was killed and the rest fled, while the Indians escaped to the mountains. Hundreds of others, some of them from the various stockades, managed also to escape to the mountains from time to time, where those who did not die of starvation subsisted on roots and wild berries until the hunt was over. Finding it impracticable to secure those fugitives, General Scott finally tendered them a proposition, through [Colonel] W. H. Thomas, their most trusted friend, that if they would surrender Charley and his party for punishment, the rest would be allowed to remain until their case could be adjusted by the government. On hearing of the proposition, Charley voluntarily came in with his sons, offering himself as a sacrifice for his people. By command of General Scott, Charley, his brother, and the two elder sons were shot near the mouth of Tuckasagee, a detachment of Cherokee prisoners being compelled to do the shooting in order to impress upon the Indians the fact of their utter helplessness. From those fugitives thus permitted to remain originated the present eastern band of Cherokees.*

---

* James Mooney, "Myths of the Cherokee," *Nineteenth Annual Report of the Bureau of Ethnology* (Washington, D.C.: Government Printing Office, 1900), 131.

as the removals began by September 1. Ross and the Emigrant Management Committee, consisting of six other Cherokees, thus organized the removal of the remaining Cherokees. The federal government provided Ross and the committee $65.88 per individual to pay for rations, wagons, horses, physicians, and other necessities.

HEADING WEST

Thirteen different detachments of Cherokees set out for Indian Territory under the guidance of the Emigrant Management Committee. The first left on September 1 and the last departed on December 5. Each detachment was supposed to include 1,000 people, though in the end they varied in size from just more than 230 to nearly 1,800. The length of their trips varied as well, though most took no less than three months. This meant that each detachment traveled and arrived in the winter months.

Ross supervised the entire operation and placed his brother Lewis in charge of providing the necessary transportation and supplies for the journey. The three detachments organized by the government in June had left from Ross's Landing. The departure points for the land routes of the 13 Ross-supervised detachments depended primarily on the location of the stockade housing of that particular group of Cherokees. Most of these parties traveled west via a northern route that made its way through Tennessee, Kentucky, southern Illinois, Missouri, and Arkansas Territory before ending at Fort Gibson (in present-day northeastern Oklahoma).

It is difficult to determine the number of Cherokee men, women, and children who died along these different trails of tears. Official statistics given by the removal conductors are not completely reliable. Scholars have estimated that, in addition to those who died prior to the journey, death from disease and exposure en route claimed more than 2,000 lives. The dead were largely those more susceptible to the

Removal in the South

Indian Territory

Ft. Gibson

Ft. Coffee
Ft. Smith

Ft. Towson

1832

Echota
1835

1830

1832

Ft. Mitchell

Mississippi R.

Routes of Removal
- - - Cherokee
- ■ - ■ ■ Choctaw
——— Chickasaw
•••••• Creek
■ - ¦ ¦ ■ Seminole
——— Converging routes
■ Fort
▲ Indian village
Indian lands before relocation with dates of cession

Note: Contemporary boundaries are provided for reference.

1832

Gulf of Mexico

0   200 miles
0   200 km

© Infobase Publishing

As this map illustrates, the approximately 16,000 Cherokees who were forced to leave their eastern home took several different routes to reach Indian Territory. However, the Cherokees were not the only people forcibly removed from their Southern home; the Choctaws, Chickasaws, Creeks, and Seminoles were all forced west by the U.S. government.

harsh conditions—children and older men and women. Hundreds of Cherokees also left their detachments and abandoned the removal. These individuals most likely returned to live in the mountains of western North Carolina and eastern Tennessee.

However, the numbers and routes of the detachments and even the number of dead do not entirely capture the history of this episode. The sentiments and experiences of those Cherokees who survived the journey remain elusive. Hired conductors and sympathetic missionaries who wrote letters to their supervisors or maintained journals wrote most records of the trail. Indeed, the recorded history of the Trail of Tears is based primarily on the writings of these outsiders.

Conductors and missionaries focused first on the elements that persistently tested the Cherokees' ability to survive. Those detachments that began their journeys in the late fall were on the road as winter weather approached. In most cases, the lack of proper clothing presented the biggest problem. Depending on the number of wagons or horses available, the Cherokees had to walk or ride, and a detachment might travel anywhere from 6 to 16 miles on a given day. Autumn rains often rendered the dirt roads nearly impassable and slowed down the removal. The onset of winter also made it difficult to ford the many rivers that crossed the paths of the Cherokee parties. A detachment could be held up for weeks under such conditions.

Reverend Daniel Sabine Butrick was a Methodist missionary who had lived among the Cherokees for nearly two decades prior to the beginning of removal. Like other missionaries in these circumstances, he chose to move west in the aftermath of the Treaty of New Echota. His detachment began its journey in early November 1838, and by late December they were near the Ohio River. The following excerpt from his journal provides a glimpse of the trail on December 28 and 29.

It is distressing to reflect on the situation of the nation. One detachment stopped at the Ohio River, two at the Mississippi, one four miles this side, one 16 miles this side, one 18 miles, and one 3 miles behind us. In all these detachments, comprising about 8,000 souls, there is a vast amount of sickness, and many deaths. Six have died within a short time in Major [James] Brown's company, and in this detachment of Mr. Taylor's there are more or less affected with sickness in every tent; and yet all are houseless & homeless in a strange land, and in a cold region exposed to weather almost unknown in their native country.[17]

Butrick's detachment completed its journey on March 24, 1839. Their removal lasted more than four months and at least 60 Cherokees died along the way.

Similar reports from other detachments presented images that were equally troubling. Disease hounded the removal parties and the bitter cold of winter made it difficult for the Cherokees to find any comfort. Some detachments spent weeks encamped along the Ohio and Mississippi rivers waiting for ice flows to melt. The ice was usually too thin to support the wagons and too thick for the bows of ferry boats. Only a thaw would make the river crossing safer for all involved. Other detachments sent small groups ahead to build fires along the route so that the Cherokees following behind could find some warmth during the course of the journey.

CHEROKEE VOICES

All of these descriptions still make it difficult to understand the true nature of the experience. When Reverend Butrick wrote in his journal that, "the little boy who died last night was buried today," it fails to give the modern reader a genuine sense of what occurred in the past. The parents of that child buried their son along the side of a road in an unfamiliar land. They could not carry their boy's body with them. Most likely they would never be able to return to visit the grave, if they even had the ability to locate it again. Due to the circumstances of the journey, they also could not have conducted a proper burial. And this is only one of the recorded deaths.

The voices of individual Cherokees are few and far between in most histories of the removal. Yet there were some who tried to describe the events. William Shorey Coodey was John Ross's nephew. In August 1840, he wrote a letter describing the departure of the first detachment organized by his uncle. About 700 Cherokees prepared to leave from their encampment just south of the Tennessee River in late September 1838. "In all the bustle of preparation," Coodey wrote, "there was a silence and stillness of the voice that betrayed the sadness of the heart."[18] Although no rain fell, thunder rolled in the distance. Coodey interpreted the sound as an ominous sign for the future of the Cherokees in the West.

Rebecca Neugin, pictured here in 1931, was three years old when she made the trip to Indian Territory in 1838. Neugin vividly remembered the prevalence of whooping cough among the emigrants and the lack of quality food.

Many memories from the Trail of Tears come filtered through age and family history. As a three-year-old in 1838, Rebecca Neugin did not have a detailed memory of her family's journey west. When she spoke of her experience years later at the age of 97, she remembered the prevalence of whooping cough among the emigrants. The weary travelers had also needed better food than the government provided. "The people got so tired of eating salt pork on the journey," she recalled, "that my father would walk through the woods as we traveled, hunting for turkeys and deer which he brought into camp to feed us."[19] Her parents walked the entire road while Rebecca, her eight brothers and sisters, and three widows and their children shared their time in the one wagon they owned.

Lillian Lee Anderson did not travel the Trail of Tears. Instead she relived the experience through the stories told by her grandfather, Washington Lee, and her aunt, Chin Deenawash. Food provided by the government was "very bad and very scarce," her grandfather told her, "and the Indians would go for two or three days without water, which they would get just when they came to a creek or river as there were no wells to get water from." Lee also never knew whether his parents died on the trail or simply got lost. He never saw them after they were forced from Georgia. Deenawash was with her husband when he died days into the journey. She was left to care for their three children. "Aunt Chin tied the little one on her back with an old shawl, took one child in her arms and led the other one by the hand," Lillian Lee Anderson said. "The two larger children died before they had gone so very far and the little one died and Aunt Chin took a broken case knife and dug a grave and buried the little body by the side of the Trail of Tears."[20]

The difficulty of the journey was further complicated at times by the actions and attitudes of white Americans living in the area. George Hicks was one of the Cherokee men chosen by Ross to lead a removal detachment. The party under his charge left on November 4, 1838, and arrived at their western destination on March 14, 1839. During their journey, these Cherokees confronted the harsh conditions presented by winter and because of ice had to wait more than two weeks before they could cross the Mississippi. Some of the most harmful events occurred within the first weeks of their journey. Hicks reported that white citizens had accosted members of the detachment and seized their horses and other goods for unjust debts. "Yet the Government says we must go," Hicks concluded, "and its citizens say you must pay me . . . and why are they so bold; they know that we are in a defenseless position."[21]

Problems also occurred with the individuals hired by the federal government to assist with the removal. John G. Burnett, a U.S. soldier on one of the detachments, knocked unconscious one cruel teamster "who was using his whip on an old feeble Cherokee to hasten him into the wagon."[22] The Cherokees also criticized the soldiers who helped in the removal process. The soldiers herded them along the muddy roads during the day and guarded them at night to make sure no Cherokee escaped. Ellis Waterkiller often heard stories from his grandmother of this brutal treatment. "Every day worse," Grandma Parsons would tell him. "Just drive um like cattle. Grandma say she walk, grandpa walk too or soldiers run bayonets through um . . . Yuh, soldiers have wagons. Feed um two times some days, sometimes feed um one time. Soldiers eat all time, take care horses better than my grandma-grandpa."[23] Grandma Parsons was one of many Cherokees who compared the soldiers' attitudes to that of farmers herding livestock.

Principal Chief John Ross traveled west with the last detachment that left Charleston, Tennessee, on December 5, 1838. The party of more than 200 individuals buried 12 of their number along the way and arrived at Fort Gibson on March 18, 1839. One of the dead was Quatie, Ross's wife. She had been in poor health prior to the journey, which is why her husband made sure they traveled by boat. Yet the cold temperatures and freezing rain were just as bad on the water as they were on land. The winter weather proved too much for Quatie and she died from pneumonia.

Her husband had little time to mourn. A little more than a month after completing the journey, Ross was busy arranging for food, clothing, and shelter for the survivors. "The health and existence of the whole Cherokee people who have recently been removed to this distant country demands a speedy remedy for the inconveniences and evils complained of,"[24] Ross wrote to U.S. officials. Instead of reflecting on his own problems, Ross worked hard to help his nation recover from the trail. And though his situation may have been the most notable because of his stature, Ross was only one among thousands of Cherokees who now had to establish a new home in the West.

CONCLUSION

From June 1838 to March 1839, nearly 16,000 Cherokees left their homelands east of the Mississippi River and traveled west. Government soldiers forced the first detachments onto flatboats and sent them on their way. The next 13 detachments also traveled involuntarily and under government supervision. They also had the logistical planning and support of Ross and the Emigration Management Committee.

Ross and the Cherokee Council had realized that they could no longer resist removal. They saw their families and relatives suffering in the stockades and knew that they had to act. In the end, it is impossible to know how many lives were saved by the determination of the Cherokee leadership to control the process after July 1838. Even their best efforts could not grant health to the feeble or immunity to the weak. Neither could they fully protect their people from the winter elements or the psychological effect.

In the fall and winter of 1838 and 1839, thousands of Cherokee men, women, and children walked, rode horses, and sat huddled in wagons. They bundled up against the rain, snow, and cold as best they could. Thousands died along the trail and were buried in graves in Tennessee, Kentucky, Illinois, Missouri, and Arkansas Territory. Those who survived would not forget. And when they arrived at Fort Gibson in present-day Oklahoma, they found themselves reunited with many of those who had set removal in motion. At the end of the Trail of Tears, the Cherokees under John Ross came face-to-face with the Treaty Party.

The Price of Cherokee Reunion in Indian Territory

On Saturday morning, June 22, 1839, four different parties of Cherokees rode to four different locations in Indian Territory. The first party of 25 headed to the home of John Ridge. Three men broke into the house, grabbed Ridge out of his bed, dragged him into the yard, and stabbed him repeatedly. He died as his wife and children watched helplessly. A second party came upon Elias Boudinot as he visited the new house he was in the process of building. Boudinot died from a series of tomahawk blows to his head. The third party ambushed Major Ridge as he rode back to his home from Arkansas Territory. Several rifle shots hit him, and his horse tossed him to the ground. He died minutes later. The fourth and final party could not find their target, so Stand Watie lived to see another day.

Although the events of June 22 happened without warning, the three deaths did not come as a surprise to the Cherokees living in Indian Territory. Many members of the recently arrived Ross party viewed the actions as executions and the logical consequence of the treaty that had led to removal. The men who died, Boudinot and the two Ridges, had each pre-dicted this outcome. They knew when they signed the Treaty of New Echota that they had quite possibly invited their demise. In December 1835, they had broken Cherokee law by ceding the tribal homelands without authority. The stated penalty was death. Nevertheless, the surviving members of the Treaty Party referred to it as murder. Watie, Boudinot's brother, called for retaliation.

A LETTER FROM JOHN CANDY TO STAND WATIE

The following letter was written by John Candy and addressed to Stand Watie. Candy had married a woman named May Ann Wa-tie and therefore was Stand Watie's brother-in-law. At the time this letter was written, Stand Watie was in Washington, D.C., lob-bying on behalf of his supporters and against the Ross party. As evidenced by Candy's report, the violence between the different Cherokee factions in Indian Territory continued to be a problem.

Park Hill, Cherokee Nation
April 10th, 1846
Dear Sir,

I promised to write to you every time anything of importance took place. After I came to the place I found out that it would hardly do to mail letters at this place, and I have had no opportunity of sending let-ters to another Post office.

You will doubtless recollect that Stand the murderer of James Starr was killed and scalped and that Faught was caught for decoying him and has since been hung. Since that time Old Cornsilk has been

The executions of these men were only the most obvious symptom of the serious problems plaguing the Cherokees in Indian Territory in the years after removal. Three different communities of Cherokees resided together in the West, and in the spring of 1839, they were not a single political entity. From June 1839 to July 1846, the leaders of these three groups struggled to coexist on their lands west of the Mississippi River. Their contest for power led to a prolonged period

killed & robbed of a negro. Mrs. Pack has had some negro children kidnapped. Barrow Justin has been caught, tried, and was hung yesterday. Ecowee became States witness against him. Bug John Brown & his company caught a horse thief and they have killed him. It is now rumored that he and his company (that is Brown) have cut up another man in Flint in his own house. Bug seems to be the Constitution, law, Court, & Executioner, Yet our Editor Can't see him in any other light than a decent & clean man, all facts to the contrary notwithstanding. I forgot to mention that another man was killed at Ellis Hardin's. This man, it is said, was one of the company in Downing's gang on the mountains. He was scalped.

I think there is now to be no end to the bloodshed, Since the Starr boys & the Ridges have commenced revenging the death of their relatives. A dozen or so are implicated and I am afraid that some of them will be more desperate than the first ones.

Murders in the country have been so frequent until the people care as little about hearing these things as they would hear of the death of a common dog. The question may be asked—Who first began the troubles in the Cherokee Nation? The answer is obvious. We know it well.

Jno. Candy

We are very anxious to hear the news.

A signatory of the Treaty of New Echota, Stand Watie was one of approximately 2,000 Treaty Party members to relocate to Indian Territory. During the Civil War, Watie raised and commanded the first Cherokee volunteer regiment in the Confederacy and was one of the last Confederate officers to surrender in June 1865.

of violent conflict over money, land, and political influence. In July 1846, however, the desire for unity finally forced a compromise. Particularly for Ross, the man who became the principal chief of all the Cherokees in the West, the need to create and maintain a unified Cherokee Nation overrode all other concerns.

CHEROKEES IN INDIAN TERRITORY

As of April 1839, three different communities of Cherokees lived in what is now northeastern Oklahoma. Although the dividing lines were not always clear, the three groups were generally referred to as the Old Settlers, the Treaty Party, and the Ross Party. Together they had to decide how best to reunite their interests. The first and most important issue was what individuals or which community would govern this western nation.

The Old Settlers were those Cherokees who had lived in the West for decades. Their numbers had grown to around 4,000 by the late 1830s. Some of these Cherokees had first crossed the Mississippi River in the 1790s, when the Spanish claimed authority over the region. Most, however, had moved west in the 1810s, when the U.S. government first began to promote removal among the Cherokees of the East. In a relatively short period of time, the Old Settlers had separated themselves from their relatives on the other side of the Mississippi. They had elected their own chiefs and established their own laws. In contrast to the developments in Georgia, these Cherokees did not have a set of written laws and had not developed a constitution. Indeed, most had moved west because they objected to the cultural changes that had occurred among the Cherokees in the Southeast.

The Treaty Party included about 2,000 men, women, and children who had journeyed west between 1836 and 1838. Led by Watie, Boudinot, the Ridges, and their allies, this group had arrived in the West and quickly made peace with the Old Settlers. They accepted the government structure already in place and lived by the established rules. Instead of worrying about western politics, these emigrants concentrated on setting up their farms and building their homes.

The last of the three groups of Cherokees, the Ross Party, was also the largest. All told, this group comprised nearly two-thirds of the Cherokee population in the West in 1839. On the one hand, Ross was concerned about the well-being of his people who had endured the brutal removal. On the other hand, he was very worried about the Cherokee government. In August 1838, the Cherokee Council in Georgia had passed a resolution stating that "the inherent sovereignty of the Cherokee Nation, together with its constitution, laws, and usages of the same are in full force and virtue and shall continue in perpetuity."[25] It was an important and forceful statement. The Eastern Cherokee leadership was determined to make sure that removal did not destroy the government and nation established by the Constitution of 1827.

To maintain this government, however, Ross first needed to establish a working relationship with the Old Settlers. In April 1839, less than one month after arriving in Indian Territory, Ross contacted John Brown, John Rogers, and John Looney, the three chiefs of the western Cherokees. He stated his belief that the eastern and western groups should hold a council to decide how to reunite as one political entity. Nearly 6,000 Cherokees gathered at the Takatoka Camp Ground on June 3. Chief Brown spoke first. He welcomed the newly arrived Cherokees even as he set the terms for their reunion. "It is expected that you will all be subject to our government and laws until they shall be constitutionally altered or repealed," the chief declared, "and that in all this you will demean [sic] yourselves as good and peaceable citizens."[26] In his brief statement, Brown made it clear that Ross and the Eastern Cherokees should submit to the authority of the Old Settlers' government.

Ross resisted this idea and Brown grew upset with the unwillingness of the new arrivals to compromise. During the next several days, the two parties tried to negotiate a settlement that would appeal to the interests of both sides. In the end, however, Brown adjourned the council even as Ross moved to call for a convention to draft a new constitution. The Old Settlers left the grounds shortly thereafter, but Ross and his followers did not end their discussions until June 21.

At the same time that Ross assumed business was done, a group of his followers decided to act on the Cherokee decree of 1829 that outlawed the sale of land without proper authority. Those who called this secret council made sure that Ross knew nothing about it. Among the names of those accused of crimes against the Cherokee Nation were the Ridges, Boudinot, Stand Watie, John A. Bell, James Starr, and George W. Adair. In each case, three men from the clan of the accused stood, declared the guilt of the individual in question, and condemned him to die. Through the selection of numbers from a hat, the council attendees chose the executioners. Allen Ross, the chief's son, received the responsibility of keeping his father occupied as the different parties carried out the sentences. All involved acted quickly and they moved to carry out the sentences of the first four men on the list the very next morning.

Although the men who planned the attacks did not include Ross in their discussions, he had to deal with the consequences of their actions. Perhaps they knew he would have disagreed with their decision. Ross was even heard to have said about Major Ridge that, "Once I saved Ridge at Red Clay, and would have done so again had I known of the plot."[27] Many doubted that the Cherokee leader had been so ignorant of events. Watie firmly believed that Ross knew about the assassinations, and from that point forward stood in violent opposition to Ross and his plans. It is reported that Watie offered anywhere from $1,000 to $10,000 for the names of those who killed his brother. He wanted revenge. Even the U.S. government was convinced that Ross had played a part in the killings. The controversial deaths of the three men therefore had the potential to undermine the negotiations for Cherokee unity in the West.

FIRST EFFORTS AT REUNION

Despite the uproar created by the deaths of the three men, Ross did not hesitate to move forward with the attempt to create a single Cherokee government. From his perspective, the longer the Cherokees remained divided, the easier it would be for U.S. officials to manipulate the situation. Ross was particularly worried that a different Cherokee government might grant final approval to the Treaty of New Echota or cede lands in the West. Ross moved quickly to broker a unified regime with the Old Settlers. He knew he had little chance to make peace with Watie and the people who were outraged by the recent killings.

Several obstacles hindered Ross's efforts to unite the rival Cherokee parties. The tensions created by the deaths of Boudinot and the Ridges were only one of the problems. The Old Settlers as well as the Watie Party were also concerned about their prospects in a unified government. Ross and his followers represented an overwhelming majority of the Cherokee population and might therefore quickly control all aspects of a reunited nation. At the same time, U.S. officials were reluctant to allow Ross to come to power since he was less likely to cooperate with the desires of the federal government.

Nevertheless, at a council held from July 1 to July 12, 1839, a group of nearly 2,000 Cherokees worked together to combine Cherokee interests. Relatively few Old Settlers attended the council, though Sequoyah and John Looney participated as prominent delegates to the council. Both men agreed with Ross that the Cherokees needed to unite to confront the U.S. government more effectively. The council attendees made a critical statement in declaring their continued belief that the Treaty of New Echota was invalid. They also drafted an "Act of Union." Sequoyah, Looney, and Ross signed this document, which proclaimed their determination to unify and operate as a single Cherokee Nation.

The council also made several decisions that only intensi-
fied the dispute between the rival factions. In one of the first
discussions of the council, those in attendance voted to par-
don any individual who had been accused of murder in the
time since the recent emigrants had arrived. The delegates
then declared that any individual who demanded revenge in
the deaths of Boudinot and the Ridges would be considered
an outlaw. Watie and his followers were given eight days to
apologize for their calls for retribution. Finally, the council
created a police force to maintain order.

The July council and the Act of Union signaled the development of a united position among the Cherokees, even
though it was responsible for initially creating more tension.
By August, Sequoyah and Looney had persuaded more Old
Settlers to accept the act and work with the Ross Party. At
the same time, the opposition to this agreement had grown
even stronger. Watie and John Rogers now led a party that
encompassed the Old Settlers and the Treaty Party. Their followers were infuriated at being labeled outlaws and viewed
the creation of the police force as a hostile act.

At the dawn of a new decade in 1840, therefore, significant
problems remained. On September 19, 1839, Ross took office
as the principal chief of the Cherokee Nation in the West. Rogers, Watie, and their respective followers continued to oppose
Ross and refused to recognize the validity of this nation formed
under the Act of Union. U.S. officials also expressed displea-
sure with the fact that Ross had done nothing to bring the kill-
ers of Boudinot and the Ridges to justice. The United States
continued to favor the Old Settlers and the Treaty Party and
did not treat Ross as the leader of a legitimate government.

CONFLICT AND THE CONSTITUTION OF 1846

From 1840 to 1846, Ross struggled against both the Cherokee opposition and U.S. officials. Ross worked hard to

convince his fellow Cherokees that it was in their best interest to unite. He also struggled to persuade the U.S. government to invalidate the 1835 treaty and negotiate a fair agreement. However, the Cherokee opposition refused to yield and U.S. officials would not consider his proposal. In the end, both Ross and his Cherokee opponents had to compromise to maintain a united Cherokee Nation. Yet Ross and his followers made the ultimate sacrifice by finally submitting to the conditions of the Treaty of New Echota.

The opposition of the U.S. government made it difficult for the newly elected Cherokee leadership to maintain its stance. Ross made his position clear. First, he led a government that represented the interests of the majority of the Cherokees in the West. Second, the United States needed to negotiate a new treaty with this government that reflected a just price for the millions of acres of land ceded in 1835. Because U.S. officials disagreed with both statements, however, Ross was in a precarious position. He had no influence in Washington and even had trouble obtaining delinquent annuity payments. The Cherokees needed this money for daily necessities and grew frustrated with Ross.

This lack of necessary funds was no small matter. The nature of removal had left the average Cherokee family with little with which to build a new life in the West. As Rebecca Neugin recalled, "Very few of the Indians . . . had been able to bring any of their household effects or kitchen utensils with them, and the old people, who knew how, made what they called dirt pots and dirt bowls."[28] Instead of the conveniences they were accustomed to using, the Cherokees from the East had to live with what they could find or make, including deer-hide leggings and raccoon-skin moccasins. Even two years after they had arrived at their new homes, a significant number of Cherokees were living in poverty. And because they had been the last to arrive, the Cherokees who had traveled the Trail of Tears in 1838 and 1839 received the inferior portions of the territory set aside for all of the Cherokees. The droughts of 1841 and 1842 only added to their misery.

Just as harmful to the lives of Cherokees in the West was the civil war that erupted from 1841 to 1846. Although U.S. officials favored the Old Settlers and their political position, the Old Settlers knew that they did not have the numbers to vote Ross out of office. Therefore, many individuals turned to violence to undermine the Cherokee government. They hoped that the resulting chaos would force U.S. officials to remove Ross from power. And while those opposed Ross initiated the violence, during the course of the five years of conflict, some of the men who supported Ross were also active participants.

Some acts of violence were isolated, and not all of those who participated did so because of politics. Many small gangs worked their way through the Cherokee lands, robbing Ross supporters out of greed. Others attacked with political purpose. James Starr, one of the men condemned to death in the secret council of 1839 for signing the Treaty of New Echota, led perhaps the most prominent of these groups that aimed to undermine Ross's position. Starr, his 6 sons, and anywhere from 50 to 60 others strived to wreak havoc in the lives of those who supported the Cherokee leader. Gangs of anti-Ross men also orchestrated a series of attacks at polling stations during the Cherokee elections in August 1843. In spite of the violence, the Ross party maintained its political position and the newly elected council quickly established a formal bodyguard for its leader. Yet many Cherokees fled the territory and settled in Arkansas to avoid the conflict.

Federal officials grew concerned about the hostilities and worked to find a solution. In 1844, President John Tyler sent a special committee to Indian Territory to investigate the situation. The committee's findings supported the position of Ross and recommended that the United States revisit previous agreements with the Cherokees and negotiate a new treaty. Tyler refused to accept these findings as definitive. Because it did not appear that the Cherokees could solve their problems, Congress passed legislation in June 1846 that formalized the split and created two distinct Cherokee nations. Although its members believed that most Cherokees wanted peace and supported Ross, Congress also assumed that the

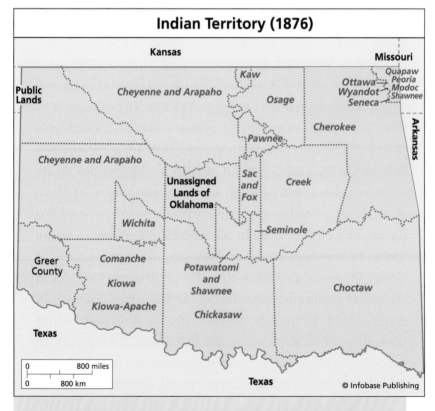

Indian Territory (1876)

In June 1846, Congress passed legislation that officially unified the three Cherokee groups in Indian Territory (present-day Oklahoma). The Cherokee Nation held a sizeable amount of land in the northeastern part of the territory (depicted here in 1876).

violence would continue unless an external force established peace.

When faced with this congressional resolution, Ross decided that he needed to compromise. For the sake of a unified Cherokee Nation, Ross negotiated a new treaty with the United States. This 1846 accord included several key resolutions. First and most important, it acknowledged the validity of the New Echota agreement and accepted the original figure of $5 million for the Cherokee lands. Second, it brought the Old Settlers and Treaty Party members into the nation and granted them per-capita payments. Third, to end the violence and any ideas regarding retribution, the treaty granted a general amnesty for all crimes committed during the previous seven years. Finally, the families of the Ridges and Boudinot received cash payments as compensation for their loss.

At the conclusion of this 1846 treaty council, Ross and Watie shook hands. Ross would continue as principal chief and Watie would continue to oppose him throughout the next two decades. The two men would not become friends, yet they were both members of a single Cherokee Nation, and that was a crucial victory. Ross made that clear when he presented the treaty to the Cherokees in November 1846. "Among the advantages derived from it may be enumerated as of special importance," the principal chief explained, "the dissolution of former parties, the renewed recognition of our government, the possession in fee of our domain unimpaired, the restoration of peace."[29] The Cherokees could now fully focus on recovering from the trauma of removal.

CONCLUSION

A host of problems confronted the Cherokees in 1839, when they arrived at their new homes west of the Mississippi River. They had just endured a traumatic journey that wrenched them from their homelands. Many families had lost loved ones on the Trail of Tears, and few people had been able to bring material belongings with them. They also faced a new environment and struggled to find suitable land on which to farm. All of this made daily life difficult and further complicated the efforts to establish new homes.

Even as individual Cherokees constantly faced these issues of survival, they also had to confront the unresolved issues that created tensions between them and those Cherokees already living in the western territories. From the spring of 1839 to the summer of 1846, the three Cherokee factions fought to resolve their differences. At stake was the right to govern the combined population of Cherokees in the West. Through it all, Ross remained steadfast. He argued for a united nation and a new treaty. Although his opponents disliked his stance and other elements of his politics, Ross never strayed from these goals. He believed that without unity the Cherokees would never fully recover or prosper. It was this belief that led him to sign the 1846 accord and surrender in the fight over the Treaty of New Echota.

Removal
and Memory

FOR MOST NON-INDIANS IN THE UNITED STATES, INDIAN removal is an unfamiliar aspect of history and merits only a short description in textbooks. But the survivors of the Trail of Tears and the descendants of those men and women have never forgotten the events of the 1830s. In 1989, the Cherokee Nation of Oklahoma observed the 150-year anniversary of the last detachment's arrival in the western territories. It was not a celebration but rather a memorial during which those in attendance recalled the tragedy and sorrow experienced by their ancestors. The Cherokee residents of northeastern Oklahoma gathered together to mark the passage of time and their presence reflected the persistence of their culture and nation.

At the time of that anniversary, Wilma Mankiller was the principal chief of the Cherokee Nation of Oklahoma. Although she believed strongly in the importance of the 1989 commemoration, she granted more historical importance to a reunion that had occurred five years earlier. In 1984, for the first time since 1838, the Cherokees from Oklahoma

Wilma Mankiller, pictured here in 2000 next to a monument honoring John Ross, was the first woman chief of the Cherokee Nation. In 1993, Mankiller was inducted into the National Women's Hall of Fame and published her autobiography, *Mankiller: A Chief and Her People*.

gathered in council with the descendants of those who had evaded removal and escaped from the Trail of Tears. The Eastern Band of Cherokees and their western relatives met in Red Clay, Tennessee, at their former council grounds. At this 1984 assembly, the Cherokees renewed ancient communal bonds and reestablished that relationship over the years since.

Both the commemoration and the reunion in the 1980s reflected a concept once expressed by author and scholar Robert Penn Warren, who noted that history "can give us a fuller understanding of ourselves, and of our common humanity, so that we can better face the future." He did not write specifically about Cherokee removal and his statement simply addresses the practice, purpose, and importance of history. Nevertheless, his thoughts are directly applicable to the manner in which the Trail of Tears has been described and remembered. Indeed, reviewing and examining events from years gone by does more than simply recount the missteps, wrongdoings, and suffering of those who lived in the past. It is an exercise that helps explain and ground the relationships in the present. And at its foundation, it is a process of memory and memorial. As Mankiller and others have expressed, the Trail of Tears must never be forgotten.

WRITTEN RECORDS AND INDIAN IMAGES

The Cherokees had not initially planned to commemorate the 150-year anniversary of the Trail of Tears. It is not easy to deal with such a tragic event from the past and they approached it with caution. However, when they learned about a group of non-Indian wagon-train hobbyists who intended to retrace the Trail of Tears, the Cherokees believed that they needed to act. Rather than see the horror of the past displayed as an adventure of the present, the Cherokees organized a memorial to honor the men, women, and children forced west in 1838.

The catalyst for and the decision to organize that memorial highlighted two important issues for the Cherokees and other Indian communities in the twentieth century. First,

WILMA MANKILLER: FIRST FEMALE CHIEF OF THE CHEROKEE NATION

In 1985, Wilma Mankiller became the first female chief of the Cherokee Nation based in Tahlequah, Oklahoma. Although she initially faced opposition because of her gender, she served as chief for 10 years. During her time in office, she focused much of her effort on improving health-care facilities and social programs for the Cherokees. She also participated in the push for increased self-determination for the Cherokees and helped her nation gain more control of funds normally distributed by the Bureau of Indian Affairs. Her work on behalf of the Cherokees gained Mankiller a national reputation as well, and she received the Presidential Medal of Freedom in 1998. Before, during, and after her time as chief, Mankiller has worked hard to protect both the future and the past of her people. In her autobiography, published in 1993, she often interweaves her personal history with that of the Cherokees as a whole. She particularly recognizes the importance of past events to Cherokees in the present. The following excerpt from her chapter on the Trail of Tears discusses the continued presence of the removal experience in the lives of Cherokees today.

I also reflect on those times before the white men and the United States government took control of our lives, when the Cherokees

the idea to retrace the Trail of Tears reflected the memory of Indian removal among non-Indians. For non-Indians, it appeared, removal was a part of distant history to be reenacted. Second, in her explanation of the memorial and the reunion, Mankiller reinforced the need for Cherokees and other Indians to take control of how their histories and images were presented to the public.

thrived in the ancient homeland of what became Georgia, Alabama, Tennessee, North Carolina, South Carolina, and Virginia. I see in my mind's eye the steady European intrusion, and how the old Cherokee people gradually blended their timeless customs with the concoctions and innovations of the whites. I visualize the events that marked those years when my people were pressured to move from the Southeast to the unknown lands west of Arkansas. Remembrances can be powerful teachers. When we return to our history, those strong images assist us in learning how not to make identical mistakes. Perhaps we will not always be doomed to repeat all of our history, especially the bad episodes.

From the annals of time, from those bittersweet years of the 1800s, the spirits of long-dead Cherokees and other native men and women from other tribes remain unsettled. Their spirits still cry out, warning us about the dangers that lie ahead. They speak of the need to read small print on documents and to search between the lines on treaties. They caution us to be aware of the droves of government bureaucrats who tend to approach native people just as those well-meaning "Bless Your Heart" ladies did in Oklahoma, the ones who tried to coax me into their big shiny cars when I was a child walking down the dirt road to school.*

---

* Wilma Mankiller and Michael Wallis, *Mankiller: A Chief and Her People* (New York: St. Martin's Press, 1993), 77–78.

In 1932, the University of Oklahoma Press published *Indian Removal,* a book written by lawyer turned historian Grant Foreman. Foreman relied on a vast array of research material to reveal how and why the U.S. government forced tens of thousands of Indians from their homes east of the Mississippi River in the early nineteenth century. It was the first comprehensive study of the experience of the Cherokees,

Choctaws, Chickasaws, Creeks, and Seminoles during the removal era. Prior to Foreman's book, the history of American Indian removal had not been a prominent element in the teaching of U.S. history.

Although *Indian Removal* capably presented the tragic impact of removal policy, it did not conclude with an image of defeated Indian communities. At the very end of the book, Foreman made a critical observation. Although devastating and deadly, removal did not represent the end of the Indians' history. Instead, the Cherokees, Creeks, Choctaws, Chickasaws, and Seminoles looked forward and faced their future west of the Mississippi River. "With this hope after their arrival," Foreman concluded, "they resolutely attacked the problems of pioneering in the strange country that confronted them." According to Foreman, the postremoval success of the Cherokees and other eastern Indians in the West "was an achievement unique in [U.S.] history."[30]

Foreman made a point of showing in that book and others that removal was not the end point of history for the Cherokee and other Indian tribes. Yet the actions of the wagon-train hobbyists in the 1980s revealed that the image of the vanishing Indian remained strong. Those who sought to reenact the Trail of Tears did so without understanding what their actions might mean to the Cherokees of the present. Indeed they may not have known that a strong Cherokee Nation remained intact and were more than capable of telling their history. Grant Foreman wrote about the survival of the Indians. For most Americans, however, the Indians had vanished.

From the perspective of the wagon-train hobbyists, retracing the Trail of Tears was not meant to be offensive. It was intended to re-create a past historical event, to journey along the route traveled by thousands of Indians 150 years before. Yet as Mankiller pointed out in her autobiography, this excursion by wagon would never capture the true

During the 150-year anniversary of the Trail of Tears in 1988, a group of wagon-train hobbyists set out to follow the path the Cherokees took to Indian Territory. However, for the Cherokees who made the trip in 1838, the journey was never perceived as an adventure.

experience. Few Cherokees who removed west had wagons. Most were lucky if they had horses, and a significant proportion completed the journey on foot. They all suffered and thousands died. At no point did the Cherokees view their removal as an adventure.

More important, though the Trail of Tears had occurred 150 years before, it was not a part of the past. The stories that were passed down within families served as a personal and living history of those events. Nannie Pierce, a Cherokee woman born in 1866, was one link in the chain that connected the Cherokees on the Trail of Tears to their descendants in the twentieth century. "I have read of the 'Trail of Tears' by different writers," she observed in a 1937 interview, "but none portray the horrors of it all in detail as grandmother related to us when we could persuade her to talk of it, as she would often tell us it was too horrible to talk about and it only brought back sad memories."[31] And for the Cherokees who now make their home in Oklahoma, their very presence in the West is a constant reminder of their expulsion from their homelands in Georgia, Tennessee, North Carolina, and Alabama. Their ancestors, those who had died along the trail and those who survived, were still very much a presence in their lives. The pain of removal, therefore, was and is fresh.

It is this truth that captures the essence of history as a record of the past. Most daily events, whether important or minor, that impact ordinary people, seldom end up in written reports. And it is also this truth that reveals the difference between the narrative of U.S. history and Cherokee memory. For most of the Cherokees who traveled along the Trail of Tears in 1838 and 1839, their personal experience is not told or remembered by American society. The Cherokee men, women, and children did not write letters, journals, or autobiographies. Therefore, even those books like Foreman's that have addressed this experience rely on the accounts of outsiders.

For Cherokees, the Trail of Tears is not a history told by outsiders. It is a living story that must be approached with care and treated with respect. In 2001, the Cherokee Heritage Center in Oklahoma presented a dramatic representation of the Trail of Tears as one way to educate the public about this history. Eastern and western Cherokees alike have also taken advantage of their tribal Web sites to present information and resources regarding the Trail of Tears and other aspects of their history and culture. Researchers and curious students can find a host of documents and historical narratives the Cherokees have placed online so that anyone who is interested can learn more about these events.

FACING THE FUTURE

Several other developments in contemporary society rein-
force this idea that the Trail of Tears is more than a tragic
event of the past. As evidenced by the reunion of eastern and
western Cherokees in 1984, the impact of the removal experience continues to reverberate in the present. The Cherokees have had to come to terms with that history and with
each other. Time has also brought to light the experiences of
a neglected portion of the Cherokee population, namely the
African-American slaves who traveled the Trail of Tears with
their Indian masters. Finally, the events of Cherokee removal
have continued to affect the ways in which the Cherokee and
other Indian nations interact with the U.S. government.

At present, there are three different federally recognized
Cherokee tribes in the United States. The Cherokee Nation
of Oklahoma is the most numerous, with a present population of more than 220,000. Although a large number of those
individuals reside in more than 14 different counties in northeastern Oklahoma, tens of thousands of enrolled members
of the nation live throughout the United States. The Eastern
Band has about 13,400 members, most of whom reside on
their land trust that encompasses 56,000 acres in the vicinity
of Cherokee, North Carolina. Finally, the more than 12,000-
strong United Keetoowah Band of Cherokee Indians is based
in Tahlequah, Oklahoma.

Relationships among these tribes in the present are still
connected to events of the eighteenth and nineteenth centuries. The United Keetoowah Band traces its traditions back
hundreds of years and its political organization to the Old
Settlers who first moved west of the Mississippi River in the
1790s and early 1800s. Keetoowah leaders continue to emphasize the importance of this band's independence, especially in
relation to the Cherokee Nation of Oklahoma. And although
members of the three recognized bands continue to meet in

Through the promotion of their culture, Cherokees are able to preserve a way of life that continues to define them today. Pictured here is tribal elder Jerry Wolfe, who is talking about his culture to two North Carolina A&T students at the Museum of the Cherokee in Cherokee, North Carolina.

council to discuss common interests, there are no plans to create a single Cherokee political entity.

The Trail of Tears narrative is also related to discussions in the present about the men and women descended from the African-American slaves of Cherokee masters. African-American slavery first became a part of Cherokee life in the late eighteenth and early nineteenth centuries as the Cherokees began to transform their society to match the expectations of U.S. officials. Prior to removal, the Cherokee government had created specific codes to govern slave behavior, and by 1835, just under 10 percent of the Eastern Cherokees owned about 1,600 slaves.

Slaves shared the bitter experience of removal and post-removal with their masters. The existence of slavery even influenced the final location of the Cherokees in the West. Federal officials made sure that the removed Indians settled south of the Missouri Compromise line in territory that allowed for the expansion of the divisive institution of slavery. However, when the Civil War brought an end to slavery in the United States, the situation among the Cherokees became more complicated. Freed African-American men and women struggled for rights and citizenship in the Cherokee Nation for decades after the end of the war. For many of their descendants, that struggle continues. Only in the past several decades have the histories of the Cherokee freed men and women received more attention.

The relationship between the Cherokees and the U.S. government also remains at its foundation a contested issue. At the center of this discussion remain the three words used by Chief Justice John Marshall more than 180 years ago. Marshall described the Cherokee and all Indian tribes as "domestic dependent nations." It was a phrase granting the Indians political independence that was at once measured and ambiguous. The term *nation* recognized the Cherokees' political government and right to rule its people. Yet the use of dependent asserted the overriding authority of the federal government in any and all matters. And forced removal appeared to confirm that power.

From 1831 to the present, the Cherokee and other Indian nations have struggled to push and better define the limits of their political independence, and the courtroom has continued to serve as a critical battleground in these efforts. The sovereignty of Indian nations like the Cherokee remains one of the most important and least understood concepts in the twenty-first century. From legal battles over religious practices to political struggles over the operation of casinos, American Indian tribes are constantly defending and promoting their right to exist as independent nations within the boundaries of the United States.

John Ross and the Cherokee Council stated in 1838 that removal would not erase the existence or authority of the Cherokee government. At the time, they were preparing to leave behind the homelands that had been ceded in a fraudulent treaty. Though facing an arduous journey and an uncertain future in the West, Ross and the Cherokees refused to surrender their autonomy. This sentiment continues today, as the Cherokee Nation of Oklahoma, the United Keetoowah Band, and the Eastern Band of Cherokee Indians continue to assert their authority over their people and homes east and west of the Mississippi River.

CONCLUSION

To the extent that history textbooks have covered the narrative of Indian removal, the Cherokee Trail of Tears has received most of the attention. There are a number of explanations for this fact. Out of any eastern Indian tribe, the Cherokee made the most organized and determined effort to avoid removal by meeting and surpassing the expectations of an outside society that wanted the Indians to change their ways. The Cherokees developed a written language, crafted a constitution, and argued their case against removal successfully in the highest court in the land. Yet still the U.S. government forced the Cherokees west. Both the tragedy of this betrayal and the devastation of the removal itself have made Cherokee history an emblematic display of the treatment of Indians in the early nineteenth century.

Yet as historian E. L. Woodward once noted, the daily lives of most people will not be recorded in the pages of documented history. Although so much has already been written about the Cherokees and the Trail of Tears, the experience of most of those who made that journey remains untold. For most Americans in the present day, the history of those men, women, and children is in the past, an appalling tale recounted briefly in history books. The connection between the past and the present is not so clear.

The Trail of Tears is not simply a piece of history to Cherokees. Nor do the horrors of that experience signal the defeat of their nation. Elizabeth Watts eloquently summed up this sentiment in a 1937 interview. "This trail was more than tears," she explained. "It was death, sorrow, hunger, exposure, and humiliation to a civilized people as were the Cherokees. Today, our greatest Politicians, Lawyers, Doctors, and many of worthy mention are Cherokees. Holding high places, in spite of all the humiliation brought on their forefathers."[32] What Watts stated in the 1930s remains true today. The descendants of those who survived the trail have always focused their efforts on building a future for their families, bands, and nations. Yet they cannot and will not forget the experiences of their ancestors. It is through the traditions, memorials, ceremonies, and successes of the present that the Trail of Tears and the struggles of the Cherokee Nation will be forever recorded, remembered, and honored.

Chronology

1773 First cession of Cherokee land in Georgia in order to pay debts owed to the state.

1776–1783 Cherokees side with British in the American Revolution; during the course of the war, American forces destroy 50 Cherokee towns.

1785 Treaty of Hopewell is signed, the first treaty between the United States and the Cherokees.

Timeline

1773
First cession of Cherokee land in Georgia

1791
Treaty of Holston

1800
Moravians establish a mission among the Cherokees

1821
Sequoyah introduces a syllabary of the Cherokee language

1827
Cherokee Nation drafts and ratifies constitution

1773   **1827**

1785
Treaty of Hopewell; first treaty between the United States and the Cherokees

1808–1810
First major western migration of Cherokees

1817
Cherokees cede land east of the Mississippi in exchange for land in Arkansas Territory

1791   Treaty of Holston is signed, in which President George Washington guarantees that Cherokee lands will never again be invaded by settlers.

1793   Georgia challenges the authority of the U.S. Supreme Court in *Chisholm v. Georgia*.

1800   Moravians establish a mission among the Cherokees.

1802   Georgia enters into compact with the United States, making the federal government responsible for terminating Indian land titles in the state.

1803   Louisiana Purchase is finalized.

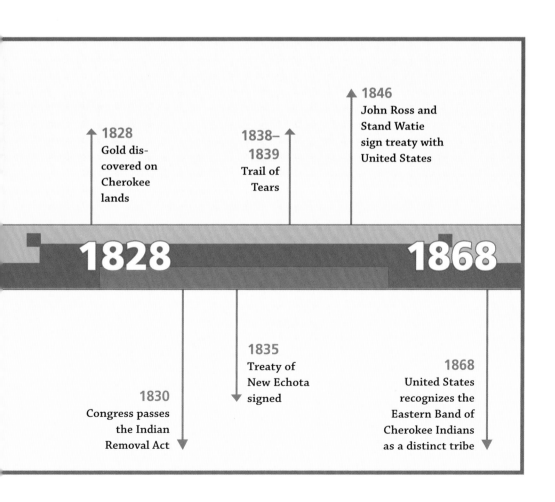

1808 First recorded law of Cherokees establishes a national police force.

1808–1810 First major western migration of Cherokees.

1810 Cherokees establish law stating that only the Cherokee government has the right to punish murderers.

1814 Cherokee warriors ally with Andrew Jackson and help defeat the Creek forces known as the Red Sticks at the Battle of Horseshoe Bend.

1817 Cherokees pass a law that grants sole authority over land cessions to the Cherokee National Council.

Cherokees sign treaty that cedes land east of the Mississippi in exchange for land in Arkansas Territory.

Missionaries from the American Board of Commissioners for Foreign Missions set up schools and missions in the Cherokee Nation.

1821 Cherokee scholar Sequoyah introduces a syllabary of the Cherokee language.

1822 Cherokee government establishes a supreme court.

1823 In *Johnson v. McIntosh,* U.S. Supreme Court rules that only Indians have a right of occupancy and the U.S. government can only obtain their land by their consent or by conquest.

1827 Cherokee Nation drafts and ratifies constitution that establishes three branches of government and declares sovereignty.

1828 *Cherokee Phoenix* first published.

Cherokees living in Arkansas Territory relocate to Indian Territory.

Andrew Jackson elected president of the United States.

Gold discovered on Cherokee lands.

1829   Georgia state legislature passes laws extending state authority over Cherokees.

1830   Congress passes the Indian Removal Act.

1831   *Cherokee Nation v. Georgia* ruling declares the Cherokee tribe a "domestic dependent nation."

1832   *Worcester v. Georgia* upholds Cherokee sovereignty and judges the Georgia laws "repugnant to the Constitution."

1835   Treaty of New Echota signed.

1836–1838   Members of the Treaty Party move west.

1838   Soldiers under the command of General Winfield Scott begin to round up the Cherokees for removal.

1838–1839   Cherokees travel westward along the Trail of Tears.

1839   Major Ridge, John Ridge, and Elias Boudinot executed for negotiating and signing the Treaty of New Echota.

Act of Union signed by John Ross and members of the Old Settlers in Indian Territory.

1846   John Ross and Stand Watie sign treaty with United States that establishes Cherokee Nation in the West and ends the violent civil war.

1861–1865   North and South fight against one another in the U.S. Civil War.

1868   United States recognizes the Eastern Band of Cherokee Indians as a distinct tribe.

1898   Curtis Act makes allotment of Cherokee lands mandatory.

1907   Oklahoma becomes a state.

1934   Cherokee Nation in Oklahoma incorporates under the auspices of the Oklahoma Indian Welfare Act.

1946   United Keetoowah Band organizes and is recognized as distinct tribe.

1976   Cherokee Nation in Oklahoma ratifies first modern constitution.

1984   Delegates from the Eastern Band of Cherokee Indians and the Cherokee Nation of Oklahoma hold council in Red Clay, Tennessee.

1989   150-year anniversary of the conclusion of the Trail of Tears.

Notes

Chapter 1

1. James Fenimore Cooper, *The Last of the Mohicans* (New York: Penguin Books, 1986), 350.
2. Reginald Horsman, *Expansion and American Indian Policy, 1783–1812* (Norman: University of Oklahoma Press, 1992), 55.
3. Francis Paul Prucha, ed., *Documents of United States Indian Policy* (Lincoln: University of Nebraska Press, 1990), 50.

Chapter 2

4. Reece letter, quoted in Theda Perdue and Michael D. Green, *The Cherokee Removal: A Brief History with Documents* (New York: Bedford St. Martin's, 2005), 48.
5. Ridge letter, quoted in Perdue and Green, *The Cherokee Removal*, 36.

Chapter 3

6. Boudinot editorial, in Theda Perdue, ed., *Cherokee Editor: The Writings of Elias Boudinot* (Athens: University of Georgia Press, 1983), 109–10.
7. Ross speech in Gary E. Moulton, ed., *The Papers of Chief John Ross, Vol. 1 1807–1839* (Norman: University of Oklahoma Press, 1985), 217.
8. Quoted in Jill Norgren, *The Cherokee Cases: Two Landmark Federal Decisions in the Fight for Sovereignty* (Norman: University of Oklahoma Press, 2004), 119.
9. Boudinot letter, in Edward Everett Dale and Gaston Litton, *Cherokee Cavaliers: Forty Years of Cherokee History as Told in the Correspondence of the Ridge-Watie-Boudinot Family* (Norman: University of Oklahoma Press, 1995), 5.

Chapter 4

10. Quoted in Perdue, *Cherokee Editor*, 225.
11. Petition, in Perdue and Green, *The Cherokee Removal*, 134.
12. Moulton, *The Papers of Chief John Ross, Vol. 1 1807–1839*, 250.
13. Quoted in Thurman Wilkins, *Cherokee Tragedy: The Ridge Family and the Decimation of a People* (Norman: University of Oklahoma Press, 1986), 263.
14. The Ridge, quoted in Wilkins, *Cherokee Tragedy*, 287.
15. The Ridge, quoted in Wilkins, *Cherokee Tragedy*, 289.

Chapter 5

16. Quoted in Vicki Rozema, ed. *Voices from The Trail of Tears*, (Winston-Salem, N.C.: John F. Blair, Publishers, 2003), 113.
17. Ibid., 147.
18. Ibid., 134.

19. Quoted in Grant Foreman, *Indian Removal: The Emigration of the Five Civilized Tribes of Indians* (Norman: University of Oklahoma Press, 1989), 302–318.

20. Interview with Lillian Lee Anderson, Volume 2, Indian-Pioneer History Collection, Archives and Manuscript Division, Oklahoma State Historical Society.

21. Quoted in Foreman, *Indian Removal*, 305.

22. "John Burnett's Story of the Trail of Tears." Available online at *http://www.cherokee. org/home.aspx?section= culture&culture=history&cat =R2OKZVC/B7c=* (accessed July 18, 2006).

23. Waterkiller interview, "Family Stories from the Trail of Tears" (Taken from the Indian-Pioneer History Collection, Grant Foreman, editor), Sequoyah Research Center. Available online at *http:// anpa.ualr.edu/digitallibrary/ Family%20Stories%20from%2 0the%20Trail%20of%20Tears. htm* (accessed July 18, 2006).

24. Letter in Moulton, *The Papers of Chief John Ross, Vol. 1 1807–1839*, 704–05.

Chapter 6

25. Quoted in William G. McLoughlin, *After the Trail of Tears: The Cherokees' Struggle for Sovereignty, 1839–1880* (Chapel Hill: University of North Carolina Press, 1993), 5.

26. Quoted in Wilkins, *Cherokee Tragedy*, 332.

27. Ibid., 339.

28. Quoted in Grant Foreman, *The Five Civilized Tribes* (Norman: University of Oklahoma Press, 1934), 283.

29. Quoted in McLoughlin, *After the Trail of Tears*, 58.

Chapter 7

30. Foreman, *Indian Removal*, 386.

31. Interview with Nannie Pierce, Volume 71, Indian-Pioneer History Collection.

32. Interview with Elizabeth Watts, Volume 95, Indian-Pioneer History Collection.

Bibliography

Cooper, James Fenimore. *The Last of the Mohicans*. New York: Penguin Books, 1986.

Dale, Edward Everett, and Gaston Litton. *Cherokee Cavaliers: Forty Years of Cherokee History as Told in the Correspondence of the Ridge-Watie-Boudinot Family*. Norman: University of Oklahoma Press, 1995.

Dowd, Gregory Evans. *A Spirited Resistance: The North American Indian Struggle for Unity, 1745–1815*. Baltimore: The Johns Hopkins University Press, 1992.

"Family Stories from the Trail of Tears" (Taken from the Indian-Pioneer History Collection, Grant Foreman, editor), Sequoyah Research Center. Available online at *http://anpa.ualr.edu/digital_library/Family%20Stories%20from%20the%20Trail%20of%20Tears.htm*. Accessed December 12, 2006.

Foreman, Grant. *Indian Removal: The Emigration of the Five Civilized Tribes of Indians*. Norman: University of Oklahoma Press, 1932.

———. *The Five Civilized Tribes*. Norman: University of Oklahoma Press, 1934.

Horsman, Reginald. *Expansion and American Indian Policy, 1783–1812*. Norman: University of Oklahoma Press, 1992.

Indian-Pioneer History Collection, Archives and Manuscript Division, Oklahoma State Historical Society.

Mankiller, Wilma, and Michael Wallis. *Mankiller: A Chief and Her People*. New York: St. Martin's Press, 1993.

McLoughlin, William G. *After the Trail of Tears: The Cherokees' Struggle for Sovereignty, 1839–1880*. Chapel Hill: University of North Carolina Press, 1993.

Mooney, James. "Myths of the Cherokee," *Nineteenth Annual Report of the Bureau of Ethnology*. Washington, D.C.: Government Printing Office, 1900.

Moulton, Gary E., ed. *The Papers of Chief John Ross, Vol. 1 1807–1839*. Norman: University of Oklahoma Press, 1985.

Norgren, Jill. *The Cherokee Cases: Two Landmark Federal Decisions in the Fight for Sovereignty*. Norman: University of Oklahoma Press, 2004.

Perdue, Theda, ed. *Cherokee Editor: The Writings of Elias Boudinot*. Athens: University of Georgia Press, 1996.

———, and Michael D. Green. *The Cherokee Removal: A Brief History with Documents*. New York: Bedford St. Martin's Press, 2005.

Prucha, Francis Paul, ed. *Documents of United States Indian Policy*. Lincoln: University of Nebraska Press, 1990.

Rozema, Vicki, ed. *Voices from The Trail of Tears*. Winston-Salem, N.C.: John F. Blair Publisher, 2003.

Wilkins, Thurman. *Cherokee Tragedy: The Ridge Family and the Decimation of a People*. Norman: University of Oklahoma Press, 1986.

Further Reading

Anderson, William L. *Cherokee Removal: Before and After*. Athens: University of Georgia Press, 1991.

Denson, Andrew. *Demanding the Cherokee Nation: Indian Autonomy and American Culture, 1830–1900*. Lincoln: University of Nebraska Press, 2004.

Ehle, John. *Trail of Tears: The Rise and Fall of the Cherokee Nation*. New York: Anchor Books, 1988.

Everett, Dianna. *The Texas Cherokees: A People Between Two Fires, 1819–1840*. Norman: University of Oklahoma Press, 1990.

Finger, John R. *Cherokee Americans: The Eastern Band of Cherokees in the Twentieth Century*. Lincoln: University of Nebraska Press, 1991.

Mails, Thomas E. *The Cherokee People: The Story of the Cherokees from Earliest Origins to Contemporary Times*. New York: Marlowe and Company, 1996.

McLoughlin, William G. *Cherokee Renascence in the New Republic*. Princeton, N.J.: Princeton University Press, 1986.

Miles, Tiya. *Ties That Bind: The Story of an Afro-Cherokee Family in Slavery and Freedom*. Berkeley: University of California Press, 2005.

Neely, Sharlotte. *Snowbird Cherokees: People of Persistence*. Athens: University of Georgia Press, 1991.

Perdue, Theda. *Slavery and the Evolution of Cherokee Society, 1540–1866*. Knoxville: University of Tennessee Press, 1979.

———. *Cherokee Women: Gender and Cultural Change, 1700–1835*. Lincoln: University of Nebraska Press, 1999.

WEB SITES

Official Site of the Cherokee Nation Based in Tahlequah, Oklahoma
www.cherokee.org/

History of the Cherokee Indians
http://cherokeehistory.com/

Official Web site of the Eastern Band of the Cherokee Nation
www.nc-cherokee.com/

National Park Service: Trail of Tears
http://www.nps.gov/trte/

Indian Pioneer History Project for Oklahoma
http://www.rootsweb.com/~okgenweb/pioneer

Cherokee History
http://www.tolatsga.org/Cherokee1.html

United Keetoowah Band of Cherokee Indians
www.unitedkeetoowahband.org/

Picture Credits

Index

About the Contributors

Author **JOHN P. BOWES** is an assistant professor in Native American history at Eastern Kentucky University. He is currently writing a book manuscript titled *Exiles and Pioneers: Eastern Indians in the Trans-Mississippi West*, which examines the removal and post-removal experience of the Shawnee, Delaware, Wyandot, and Potawatomi Indians from the late 1700s to the 1870s. The book will be published by Cambridge University Press as part of its series Studies in North American Indian History. Bowes received a B.A. in history from Yale University and completed both his M.A. and Ph.D. in history at the University of California at Los Angeles.

Series editor **PAUL C. ROSIER** received his Ph.D. in American history from the University of Rochester in 1998. Dr. Rosier currently serves as assistant professor of history at Villanova University, where he teaches Native American history, the environmental history of America, history of American Capitalism, and world history. He is the author of *Rebirth of the Blackfeet Nation, 1912–1954* (2001) and *Native American Issues* (2003). His next book, on post-World War II Native American politics, will be published in 2008 by Harvard University Press. Dr. Rosier's work has also appeared in various journals, including the *Journal of American History,* the *American Indian Culture and Research Journal,* and the *Journal of American Ethnic History.*